MANAGEMENT PLUS™

Maximizing Productivity through Motivation, Performance, and Commitment

Robert A. Fazzi, Ed. D.

IRWIN
Professional Publishing
Burr Ridge, Illinois
New York, New York

Senior sponsoring editor: Cynthia A. Zigmund
Project editor: Stephanie M. Britt
Production manager: Jon Christopher
Designer: Heidi J. Baughman
Art manager: Kim Meriwether
Art studio: Graphics Plus
Compositor: TCSystems, Inc.
Typeface: 11/13 Palatino
Printer: Book Press, Inc.

Library of Congress Cataloging-in-Publication Data

Fazzi, Robert A.
　　Management Plus : maximizing productivity through motivation, performance, and commitment / Robert A. Fazzi.
　　　　p.　　cm.
　　Includes bibliographical references and index.
　　ISBN 1-55623-756-1
　　1. Personnel management.　　2. Supervision of employees.
　　3. Employee motivation.　　4. Labor productivity.　　I. Title.
　　HF5549.F35　　1994
　　658.3—dc20　　　　　　　　　　　　　　　　　　　　93–37972

Printed in the United States of America

2 3 4 5 6 7 8 9 0 *BP* 0 9 8 7 6 5 4

To my mother Helen M. Fazzi and my father Aldo J. Fazzi, whose lives reflect the caring, compassion, sensitivity, and love that are at the foundation of healthy families and a healthy world.

Preface

This may be the most concise, concrete, and helpful management book you will ever read. It is designed to do one thing—provide you with decisive answers on how you can most effectively supervise, motivate, and gain the enthusiastic commitment and support of each person you supervise.

This book is written for people who want to be exceptional managers.* It is not a philosophical book or one that loses the reader in theory. It does not focus on leadership traits or qualities. Nor is it saturated with the latest management techniques. And it certainly will not present ambiguous management suggestions like "be empathic" or "be responsive."

Instead, this book responds to the number one reality that affects a manager: You are responsible for getting the job done. And getting the job done must be accomplished by the people you supervise. Specifically, this book presents the newest, most effective model available for you to supervise, motivate, and gain the maximum performance and commitment from every employee.

Of course, management theory and philosophy, leadership traits, and management techniques remain important and play critical roles in the development of a manager. But they certainly are not the top priorities of a manager struggling to find a better way to supervise and motivate specific employees. Managers need concrete answers, not theory, to the real problems of supervising and managing people in today's complex business world.

The model in this book provides clear answers to three key supervisory questions.

---

* Throughout this book, the term *manager* refers to anyone who is responsible for supervising and managing staff.

- What is the most effective supervisory approach to use with each staff person?
- Why is a particular approach effective? The logic of the model will help you learn quickly why it supports what you do.
- How is the model most effectively used with each employee you supervise?

THE REALITY OF PERSONNEL MANAGEMENT

To those who manage people, one thing is consistently clear: Staff is different. Some members of your staff may be of the same age, sex, or race. All may have had the same training or education. They may even have been hired on the same day. Despite similarities, you know for certain that they often differ significantly in skill and motivation.

Think about the people you supervise. While you may like and respect each of them, isn't it true that each has a different performance level? A number of employees may be high performers who always do a great job and are highly reliable.

Other members of your staff may have the skills to do the job. They may even have been outstanding performers in the past, but for some reason now lack motivation and seem bored. They could be burned out. Another group of employees may not have the skills to do the job, yet are highly motivated and want to improve their overall performance.

And then there are the employees who simply don't come through. Despite all your encouragement and support, they seem unable to master the basic skills needed to do the job. They may lack not only the skills but also may seem unconcerned or unmotivated.

If you think about it, your employees probably perform at a wide range of levels. It makes no sense to use the same managerial and supervisory approaches with each person. Imagine how your high performers would feel if you treated them the same way that you treated the low performers.

Once managers accept and understand the fundamental differences and individuality of their employees, they can begin to look for approaches that deal effectively with the whole spectrum of employees. The model is comprehensive enough to include all types of employees and simple enough to be easily learned and applied. Above all, it is a model that works.

RESPONDING TO TODAY'S MANAGEMENT REALITIES

This book is based on two important premises. First, employees must be treated with dignity and respect. Second, effective supervision and management are critical to the functioning of the organization.

Before accomplishing anything else, managers must first provide their employees with a work environment where they are treated with the respect and dignity that they need and deserve. A manager who fails to do this should not look for respect in turn. Employees who do not respect the manager are likely to lack respect for the job as well. Perhaps the company as whole may suffer.

Managers need to understand the importance of the role employees play within the organization. The success or failure of modern business depends on how managers encourage optimal performance by their employees. If they are successful, the organization is in a position to thrive. If they fail, the organization will never have a chance.

Managers act as catalysts in converting organizational philosophy, mission, and strategy into reality. They hire, support, motivate, and empower staff; encourage increased productivity; develop teams; monitor performance; and do hundreds of other things to ensure that products or services are provided in a timely and qualitative manner.

Unfortunately, managers seeking guidance often learn a lot more about the philosophy of management than the reality of management. They can search for excellence, commit themselves to total quality management, service America—and do it all in one minute. But if employees become disillusioned, are unproductive, and lose their commitment to the organization, managers face big trouble. All the kings' horses and all the kings' philosophers won't put their businesses together again.

OVERVIEW OF THE BOOK

The book is designed to systematically build upon the information you need to learn and apply the model effectively.

Chapters 1 and 2 provides the background, rationale, and key components of an ideal supervisory management model. It also identifies the six goals of supervision and reviews why managers must achieve all six goals.

Chapter 3 reviews the three major supervisory behaviors that managers must use with employees. It also provides a number of particularly effective, proven management skills.

Chapter 4 focuses on an objective means to assess the functioning level of individual employees. It presents a logical, easy-to-learn management tool for doing this. Once you know how to assess the functioning level of employees, you can determine how to best supervise and motivate them.

Chapter 5 brings chapters 2 and 3 together by presenting a comprehensive Functional Management Model that provides a framework and guidelines for determining the most effective ways to supervise employees. A graphic presentation of the model makes it easy to understand and appreciate.

Chapters 6–9 focus on how to apply the Functional Management Model to various types of employee problems. It analyzes four major types of employee problems and develops strategies that define the best way to respond to each problem. Case studies are drawn from real-life.

Chapter 10 is for you, the manager. It provides a step-by-step process to deal with the most challenging employees. You will be asked to focus on the most challenging staff person and then shown how to systematically determine the employee's functional level and how to apply the model to determine the best supervisory approach.

Chapter 11 summarizes the questions asked most frequently about the model.

Following Chapter 11 is a bibliography of helpful works on supervisory and personnel management. It favors practical books that are responsive to the most common management challenges.

BEFORE STARTING THE BOOK

Perhaps the biggest challenge in writing this book was trying to restrain my enthusiasm for the Functional Management Model. I wanted to present the information as objectively as possible, without injecting any bias for the model, but I believe so deeply in the logic and effectiveness of the model that it is impossible to conceal my exuberance for it. When you finish this book, I am confident that you will share this exuberance.

What you are about to learn comes from more than 20 years of researching, managing, and training managers at all levels and in all industries. Experience and feedback from managers across the country have shown that this model works and works consistently.

When the workshop training stops and managers return to their organizations, they face reality: a range of employees who need supervision, motivation, and support. This book deals with that reality.

Acknowledgments

The development of Management Plus™ and the new Functional Management Model is the result of the support, guidance, and challenges of a large number of colleagues, family, and friends.

This book reflects the input and insights of thousands of participants in workshops throughout the United States who have constantly pushed for further refinement of the principles that underscored the application of Management Plus™. They helped me to better understand how the model would be used and what was necessary to make the model more user-friendly.

My colleagues in the field of management and human development played a big role. Bob Agoglia, Maureen Skipper, Hal Gibber, Kay Wright, Diana Buckley, Andy Phillips, Stephanie O'Donnell, Elaine Bartro, Cindy McCrum, Gloria Powaza, John Paul Morsey, Bill Lyttle, and Carl Townsend provided both inspiration and real-life experiences that helped to further refine the model. The creativity and dedication of Jim Herlihy, Dick Murphy, and Bruce Hildreth showed that there were numerous ways of solving problems.

Steve McCafferty, Betsy Loughran, Jim Goodwin, Sandra Jacobs, Bob Brick, Ronn Johnson, and the nearly 100 directors, supervisors, and managers of the Center for Human Development continually demonstrated the ability to motivate staff and gain their support and commitment even in highly regulated environments.

Mary Giarrusso typed many versions of the manuscript and did it with a smile even as deadlines approached. Tony Giarrusso saved the day numerous times and proved that with the Mac anything could be done. Dave Martel provided legal support on the trademark issues and Bob Hatheway helped establish a working relationship with Irwin Professional Publishing. And, of course, thank you to Cindy Zigmund, that kind, gentle, supportive editor from Irwin Professional Publishing who proved that even people with soft voices can get reluctant writers to sit at the computer and finish their task.

Finally, my sincere thanks to my three daughters Jennifer, Jill, and Sarah—each of you is a joy, a challenge, and an inspiration.

Contents

Chapter Eight
THE RELUCTANT PERFORMER: THE F-3 EMPLOYEE/HIGH ABILITY/LOW MOTIVATION   136

Chapter Nine
THE MODEL EMPLOYEE: THE F-4 EMPLOYEE/HIGH ABILITY/HIGH MOTIVATION   155

Chapter Eleven
QUESTIONS AND ANSWERS: RESPONDING TO QUESTIONS PEOPLE ASK MOST 192

Chapter One

The Need for a New Supervisory Management Model
One that Works

T he need for effective supervisory management knows no boundaries. It doesn't matter if you are a first-time supervisor, a seasoned midmanager, or the president of the company. It doesn't matter if you work for a multinational Fortune 500 company, a state agency, a small business firm, a nonprofit agency, a hospital, or any one of thousands of public or private businesses found throughout the world.

It doesn't even matter if you are a relatively new entry to the labor force or a seasoned veteran, man or woman, or belong to one of the many nationalities in the workforce. If you are a manager who supervises people, your success or failure depends on how well you are able to supervise, motivate, and gain the commitment of the people you manage.

While there is tremendous focus on the continuing evolution of philosophical approaches to management—most recently total quality management—there is little focus on how managers can work and supervise individual employees more effectively. Recent trends in how organizations should be run are important, and the new emphasis on total quality management has provided solid guidelines for the development of high-quality organizations.[1] Most managers will support any efforts that will improve the quality, productivity, and viability of their organization. But they also know that the most effective approaches to modern management call for the strong involvement and empowerment of the

1

employees of the organization in addition to the development of a clear, compelling organizational vision.

These concepts initially may have been difficult for some managers. Giving employees more control can cause some managers to feel threatened. But most quickly recognize the value of empowering and involving employees in addressing problems, improving organizational functioning, and shaping the future of the organization. Managers know that the more employees have a sense of ownership in the company, the more they will be committed to doing what they can to ensure its success. John Dunlop, secretary of labor under President Ford and a professor at Harvard University, is a serious student and commentator on labor and management. Dunlop believes that many managers, particularly corporate managers, fail to recognize the value of employee contributions and the importance of allowing them a stake in the future of the company. "You have to pay attention to human resources," he says, "or it will come back to bite you."[2]

Within the organization, managers at all levels are most responsible for gaining the active involvement of employees. They take the vision of the organization and work with employees to make that vision a reality.

KEY QUESTIONS FROM MANAGERS

Managers committed to doing an excellent job have many important questions. What is the best way to work with each employee? How can they support and motivate them? Given all the demands that employees face, what is the best way to empower employees and encourage their active involvement in their work? How should managers approach the challenge of helping employees improve their performance, commitment, and morale? What can the manager do to help each employee feel committed to the vision of the agency and feel that he or she is an important part of the organization's future?

The questions may be simple, but the answers are more complex. Managers realize that they cannot use the same approach with every employee. A manager must respond differently to a superstar veteran than to a new or struggling employee. Yet little guidance is available to managers about working with employees and helping them become an active part of the mission of the organization.

If you are really committed to being an ideal manager and helping your employees reach their full potential, how do you go about it? If you are like most managers, you will seek guidance from the latest answers to the age-old problems at your local bookstore. As you turn your head sideways to read the titles on the shelves, you discover three kinds of books: books that advocate a certain philosophy of management, books that advise how to be a better leader, and books that offer the latest techniques on optimal management.

THE NEED FOR A SUPERVISORY MANAGEMENT MODEL

Each type of book provides managers with important insights. For managers interested in moving up, they provide a foundation and guidelines for approaching the overall challenge of running and managing an organization.

These books rarely respond to the one concrete problem faced by managers at all levels—how to effectively supervise and motivate staff. Managers are still left with the same questions.

- How do I supervise staff who are functioning at different levels?
- Why can't I get this employee motivated?
- How do I keep my highest-functioning employees enthusiastic?
- Are there specific supervisory approaches I should be using?
- Are there specific supervisory guidelines I should be following?
- What should I do if nothing seems to work?

Supervisors and managers face these questions every day. When they are on the line and facing the reality of trying to motivate a specific employee, they don't need theory; they need a practical, workable approach to supervising and motivating staff. The question remains, "Is such a practical, effective model available?"

Fortunately, the answer is an emphatic yes. A comprehensive supervisory management model that integrates the best components of former models with contemporary research and theory has emerged over the past 20 years. The model has been taught to and used by thousands of managers in public and private organizations. Most important, the model has proved effective with employees at all levels of functioning. The model—the focus of this book—is called the Functional Management Model.

Before moving forward, it is important to develop a clear understanding of what is meant by supervisory management model.

What Is a Supervisory Management Model?

A supervisory management model is different from management philosophy, which is a set of leadership traits or management techniques. Rather, it is a set of comprehensive principles or guidelines that provide the conceptual framework that defines how managers can supervise and motivate their employees most effectively.

Comprehensive means that the model must incorporate the supervisory needs of the full range of employees that are supervised. The model must be able to provide direction for dealing with low- or high-functioning employees. If it does not apply to all employees, it is not a complete model and is probably not very helpful.

Further defined, a supervisory management model is logical and incorporates solid management theory and research. It must make sense to the person learning the model and must provide guidelines that are clear and responsive to the supervisory realities that the manager faces. By our definition, a supervisory management model would be

A comprehensive set of logical principles and guidelines that provide managers with a conceptual framework that clearly defines the specific supervisory approaches and strategies that they should use with each employee. The model must provide managers with the guidelines needed to gain optimal levels of performance, motivation, and commitment from each person that they supervise.

The model must answer three key supervisory management questions:

1. What is the best way to supervise each of my employees?
2. Why should I do it that way? (What is the logic that supports this approach?)
3. How can I most effectively apply this supervisory approach?

If the model is effective, the answer to the "why" question substantiates "what" should be done. If the answer to the "why" question is logical, you will feel confident and comfortable with your supervisory decision. If you feel comfortable with the rationale provided by the model, how you apply it will become more apparent and easier to learn.

Defining the Optimal Supervisory Model

Now that a model has been defined and you have a better understanding of what it means, the second question to answer is, "What does a supervisory management model need to have to be an optimal model?"

To be truly responsive to your needs as a manager, a model like the Functional Management Model must incorporate 10 critical components. The ideal model must be

1. *Comprehensive.* The model must address all of the supervisory needs of all the staff that you supervise. If the model works only with staff who are highly motivated or highly skilled, then it will not respond to the staff who are neither.

On the other hand, if a model provides you only with direction on how to deal with problem employees, it will fail to provide you with the guidance needed to keep your higher functioning employees excited and motivated to do a high-quality job.

In reality, you have many different kinds of employees. If the model is going to help you, it must be comprehensive and capable of providing you with clear direction on what you need to do with all of your employees. You may be uncertain about how to supervise only one employee, but this person may cause you a tremendous amount of concern and frustration. A truly comprehensive model will provide guidance on what to do with that employee.

> **2. *Individually oriented.*** The model must not only include all employees but also provide guidance on how to assess the functional level of each of them. It should show you how to individualize your supervisory approach to respond to the unique needs and realities of each employee. In short, it should provide the framework on how to best supervise and motivate each employee.

It may sound good at first to focus on providing a consistent type of supervision to all employees. You've heard people say that the best supervisors are those who are consistent. "They treat everyone the same." "They don't play favorites." "It doesn't matter if you've been there 10 days or 10 years, they won't be unfair to anyone."

It sounds good . . . but it doesn't make sense. You can be fair to everyone, but that doesn't mean that you should treat everyone the same. Would it be logical, for example, to focus supervision and support on the employee who has been with you for 10 days in the same way that you support the employee who has been with you 10 years? The first will need support in training and orientation. The second will need supervisory support directed at helping maintain the excitement and commitment to doing the job in a timely and qualitative manner. The challenges in supervising and supporting a new employee are obviously much different than those associated with a seasoned veteran.

An ideal supervisory management model must account for this reality. It must provide the guidelines for assessing the functional level of any employee. It also must provide the framework needed for determining the best supervisory approach for each person you supervise. Essentially, the ideal model gives you a clear understanding of how to individualize your supervisory approach and how to motivate and encourage optimal performance from all of your employees.

> **3. *Flexible and capable of responding to changing employee realities.*** Do you want all of your employees to maintain their level of performance? If they are all high performers, the

answer is yes. But what if they are not? You certainly don't want to see employees maintain a less than adequate level of performance. What do you do? You help the lower-level performers improve their skills and motivation so that they ultimately become high-level performers.

For the model to be effective, it must not only allow you to differentiate between lower and higher functioning employees; it must also be flexible enough to allow you to revise your supervisory management approach toward employees who are changing their overall level of functioning. When this happens, the model should provide you with guidance for when and how to modify your level of supervision.

What about employees who were high performers but now appear to be losing their enthusiasm and commitment? Should you continue to supervise them the same way? Doesn't the fact that they are not performing at their previous standards suggest that you need to do something different? Of course! Once again, if the model is truly effective, it will provide you with the flexibility, insight, and guidelines needed to adjust your supervision of an employee based on that employee's level of performance. The model must incorporate planned flexibility with guidelines for adjustments to your supervisory approach.

4. *Encourage and ensure skill development of each employee.* As a manager, you know that the work must be done well and on time. Each employee must learn the skills necessary to do a job well and within a predefined time. The worker on the automobile assembly line and the nurse in the emergency room must learn certain skills. Even if they possess the proper skills, they still need to apply these skills in a timely fashion for the work to be acceptable. For the assembly line worker, lack of the ability to combine quality and timeliness could result in a defective automobile; for the nurse it could mean life or death for patients in the emergency room.

Managers are responsible for ensuring that their staff learn the skills needed to do their job in a qualitative and timely fashion. The model must provide managers with direction on how to define and support the development of appropriate skills by each employee. It must ensure that managers focus their time and energy in supporting task and skill development for employees who are in the learning stage of their jobs.

5. *Encourage the motivation of each employee.* It is not enough that your employees have the skills to do the job. It is equally important that they be motivated to do it. You don't want a situation in which talented employees come through only when you are standing over them. You want employees who possess enthusiasm, commitment, and initiative all the time.

One thing you know for sure is that you have different types of employees. Some are extremely motivated. They arrive early for work. They're constantly trying to learn new skills. They're reliable. These employees always come through. Other employees, unfortunately, are much less motivated. They may have the skills but seem to lack interest in doing the job unless they are pressured to do it. Although you know that they can do the job, you can't rely on them.

A truly effective model must provide guidance on how to motivate different types of employees. Because they differ, how you motivate each of them may not be the same. The model must provide a framework and clear understanding of how to determine an employee's motivational needs and how to implement strategies that respond to those needs.

6. *Encourage the personal and professional development of each employee.* As Bob Dylan once sang, "The times they are a changing." Today, employees are looking for more in their jobs than a paycheck. They want to belong to an organization that cares about them as people and as professionals.

In the past, employers were little concerned about the personal and professional development of their employees. Employers believed that a fair exchange existed between employee and employer. The employee gave a fair day's work and the employer gave a fair day's pay. Why did employers need to be concerned about anything else?

Today, the exchange is more complicated than that. Employees give more than a fair day of work. They give their commitment, their enthusiasm, their creativity, and much of themselves. The better they feel about the place where they work, the more intense that enthusiasm and commitment will be. The challenge facing managers is to nurture these positive attitudes.

Frank Popoff, president and chief executive officer of the Dow Chemical Company, says succinctly, "The professional development and management of our human capital must be the first priority of today's manager. The organization that encourages people development as a premier priority will excel in today's competitive environment." Popoff adds, "People and technology have eclipsed raw materials and energy in industries' drive for excellence."[3]

We all prefer to work in positions where our employers are genuinely concerned about our personal and professional development. P. Ranganath Nayak is senior vice-president of the Arthur D. Little, Inc., think tank in Cambridge, Massachusetts. He is in charge of corporate marketing and worldwide management productivity. "Employees," says Nayak, "need to feel that their contributions are recognized, valued, and appropriately compensated, just like managers, welders, and word processors want more than cash from their jobs. Appropriate compensation includes recognition, a measure of job security, and a voice in decisions that affect the worker."[4]

For the model to be effective, it must respond to this reality by providing guidance on creating an environment where staff feel supported. An optimal supervisory management model must provide managers with a clear sense of when and how to focus on the personal and professional development of employees. It should also show how this focus will increase employee morale, commitment, and motivation.

> 7. *Support team development.* If you have been a manager for
> even a short period of time, you know that teams are the
> building blocks of organizations. Employees work both as
> individuals and as members of a team. The worker on the
> assembly line and the nurse in the emergency room are
> members of teams. Their effectiveness often depends on the
> effectiveness of other members of the team.

As a manger, you must be concerned with the individual development of each of your employees. You must ensure that your employees have the proper skills to do the job. You must initiate efforts to ensure that they are motivated to do their jobs in a timely and qualitative fashion. And you must recognize that employees are more satisfied with and committed to an organization that responds to their personal and professional needs. However, because employees rarely work alone, you must also expand the focus of these efforts from the individual to the group.

Today managers must be concerned about the development of the team of employees. As a manager, you are likely to be evaluated on the functioning of all the members of your team. Many times the success of individual members depends on close working relations and coordination among team members. It is part of your job to ensure that there is smooth coordination and strong team spirit among all members of your team.

Coordination simply means that roles are clear and the interaction among members flows smoothly and effectively. Team spirit is a little harder to measure. Team spirit is a feeling. When team spirit is high, your team is seen as a great group with whom to work. When team spirit is low, employee morale and work satisfaction suffer. A team member may be functioning at a high level but hate working on the team. You suddenly become the department or unit that staff hates to work for. What would it take for people to leave your team? If the answer is one dollar, you have a problem. And if team members would accept a cut in pay to leave—it happens sometimes—you are in deep trouble.

An optimal model needs to address this reality by providing the manager with insights on how to make the overall team a positive and supportive place. The more positive and supportive your team is, the better it feels to be a member of it. And the better employees feel about their team, the more committed they are to the mission and goals of your department or unit. The model must provide a clear understanding of what you can do to help enhance overall team performance.

8. *Learn from the strengths and failures of previous models.* The Functional Management Model is incredibly responsive and effective, but it is not the first management model ever developed. University libraries are filled with journals that track the evolution of every segment of the field of management, including personnel management. Much has been learned over the years, particularly that the better models tend to build on those aspects of older models that have proved to be consistently effective, while adding new dimensions that address the weaknesses of earlier models.

It makes absolutely no sense to present a new management model that does not recognize the strengths of earlier models. A truly effective new model must integrate the proven strengths of earlier models with contemporary management research and practice, and it should overcome their acknowledged weaknesses. The Functional Management Model has been painstakingly responsive to this reality.

9. *Adaptable to all types of businesses and all fields.* For the new model to work, it must be applicable to more than one or two fields. If the principles are sound and the conceptual framework is well supported, the model should be as applicable to the manufacturing industry as it is to the service industry. It should be as helpful to a manager who supervises employees on the assembly line or in maintenance as it is to a manager working with employees in the insurance, banking, food, or retail industries. It should work as effectively in the public sector as in the private sector. It should work as effectively for managers in large organizations as for those in small organizations. It should work as effectively for men as it does for women.

Does this mean that the model will be used in every industry or by each manager in exactly the same way? Of course not. While many similarities are usual within industries, major differences often exist between industries. Salary structures and reward systems in one retail store often parallel those of other stores. But between industries not only are the salary, benefit, and reward systems vastly different, but also employee expectations may differ dramatically. There could be major differences in education, work hours, training time, and risk. All affect how managers might relate to their employees.

An effective model, however, will provide managers with direction and clarity on the best way to supervise each employee within the realities of each organization. An effective model will also allow managers to integrate industry-specific reward and motivational approaches with a logical and consistent framework for applying those approaches. It will work effectively within the realities of each industry and will allow the manager to apply highly effective strategies for supervising each employee within the framework of the model.

10. *Be practical, functional, and responsive to the realities of management.* If this list of 10 critical components of an ideal model had been presented in a strict priority, this

component would be first on the list. If the model is to be effective, it must be user-friendly. Managers don't want a model that is difficult to understand and even harder to apply. They want a model they can easily understand, that is practical, and that is responsive to all employee management challenges. It needs to be logical and make sense. The more logical the model is to you, the more confident you will be in using it. Most important, it has to be a model that works and works consistently.

A one-word definition of the greatest strength of the Functional Management Model is *practical*. This model works. As soon as you learn the concepts and guidelines of the model, you will be able to use them and apply them to every employee under your supervision.

Thousands of people have been trained in the Functional Management Model, including public and private employees, people with less than a high school education, and people with post-doctorate degrees. Some have been managers for more than 30 years while others have just become managers. Trainees range from supervisors, midmanagers, and senior managers to company presidents and CEOs. Some have been trained in the model in small groups; others have attended sessions with 500 or more people. They live and work in urban, suburban, and rural areas. Some supervise a small staff while others supervise large numbers of people. It doesn't matter who they are, where they work, or how they learned the model—one thing remains the same: They praise the practicality of the Functional Management Model. "This Model is wonderful. It works. I applied it immediately when I got back to my organization. I now know what to do and how to supervise each of my employees more effectively."

For the Functional Management Model to truly work, it must provide you with a logical rationale for how to manage each of the employees that you supervise. Its logic should make sense. The model also should provide you with practical and easy-to-apply guidelines. Finally, the model should work consistently with any employee.

Chapter Two

Supervisory Management: What Is It?

The Functional Management Model, the newest, most effective supervisory management model, will unfold in the next few chapters. You will learn the knowledge and skills essential to ideal supervisory management. In this chapter, you will learn the answers to three critical questions:

1. What is ideal supervisory management?
2. What major goals must all managers have when supervising staff?
3. What behaviors must managers learn in order to achieve those goals?

Before you can take even a small step toward becoming an ideal supervisory manager, you must understand clearly what is meant by the term *ideal supervisory management.* Approach the answer to this question the same way organizations approach strategic planning. If you were involved in an organization's strategic planning, the first question you probably asked yourself was, "What is my vision of an ideal organization?" What this question really asks, however, is, "What is my definition of the ideal organization?"

This is a critical question for an organization because the answer often provides the parameters and direction for overall planning. If the planners know what the ideal is, they can begin to determine how the organization can move to that ideal state. In essence, organizational planners are saying, "If we know where we are going, we will know how to get there." The same is true for supervisory management.

DEFINING SUPERVISORY MANAGEMENT

Ideal supervisory management involves both the quality of the relationship and degree of support that a manager provides the people he or she supervises. These two elements are at the heart of the organizational structure and chain of command. If they work well, the organization works well. If they don't, the organization may be in trouble.

Think about how many definitions you had to learn in your subjects at school. How many can you remember today? Not many, I'm sure. So, why is it necessary for you to have a clear definition of supervisory management? For one simple reason: Each segment of the definition addresses a specific aspect of what you need to understand to become an effective manager. Miss a segment and you weaken your potential to excel as a manager. Let's look at the key sections that need to be incorporated in defining supervisory management.

An Ongoing Process

The management of staff is not a one-shot deal. Just because you did a great job supervising an employee today doesn't mean you will have no worries about that employee tomorrow. You may have accurately assessed how well a particular employee is functioning and identified barriers affecting that employee's performance. You may have come up with some highly effective strategies to energize that employee to achieve a higher level of performance. But your responsibilities don't end here.

Ideal supervisory management is ongoing. Ongoing means that you continue to monitor how your employees are functioning. It means you continue to use your knowledge and skills to guide employees so they can perform at an optimal level. What issues are they dealing with? What are their personal and professional needs? What changes do you notice? Does their performance suggest that you alter your supervisory approach? What is a specific employee doing that should be praised, corrected, or responded to?

The art of supervising staff is dynamic, not static. Your employees are constantly changing. Ideal supervisory management means that the manager recognizes the dynamic and constantly evolving relationship between manager and employee.

Striving for Optimal Levels of Functioning from Each Employee

A manager's goal is to help everyone he or she supervises achieve an optimal level of performance, nothing less. One of the most important things that managers do is to set expectations. If you expect mediocre performance from an employee, that is the best you will get. At the same time, expecting an exceptional level of performance doesn't mean you will get it. But you are sending a message to your employees that you believe in them as individuals and believe they are capable of performing at high levels.

What happens if you send employees a different message—one that says you believe they are capable of only being mediocre? Will they strive to excel? Will their confidence level be affected by the fact that you don't expect much from them?

A better way to look at this is to look at yourself. Assume that you can choose one of two managers for whom to work. Both are kind, admirable people. One has low expectations of employees; the other has high expectations. Who would you choose? Most people would certainly prefer the manager with the higher expectations. Why? Because most people prefer to work for someone who believes in them and believes that they have the talent and drive to excel.

Your attitude as a manager is powerful. Participant managers in the training programs were asked to identify the one person who had the greatest impact on their development as a manager. People named parents or significant relatives, teachers, or one of their managers, very often their first manager.

They were next asked how the person they named helped in their development. A response that always came up was that the person "believed in them." Participants often said:

"She believed that I could do it. Even when I became discouraged, she always expressed the belief that I could do it."

"He gave me the confidence to believe in myself."

"He provided the support and guidance that helped me learn the skills that I needed. At all times, he expressed the firm belief that I had the potential and talent to learn the job."

"She saw inner strength and talent that I sometimes didn't know was there. She helped me to soar by believing that I had the potential to do almost anything."

The people named by the managers all had one thing in common: they believed in the managers and helped the managers believe in themselves. The result? Employees who gained the confidence to achieve an optimal level of functioning.

Focusing on Individual and Team Performance

Managers work with individuals. Individuals work on teams. Managers are responsible for teams of individuals. Therefore, ideal supervisory management responds to both individuals and the team.

You need to practice ideal supervisory management to help each of your employees achieve the optimal level of functioning and performance. But managers work not only with individual employees but also with individuals who make up a team. It could be an audit team in an accounting firm, a nursing team in a visiting nurse agency, the team of waiters and waitresses in a restaurant, or the team of employees working on a shop floor. The team, unfortunately, is often overlooked.

Today teams are the building blocks of organizations. Within the total quality management movement, the team is often the focus for all change.

Edward E. Lawler III recognizes the growing importance of teams in the workplace. Lawler is director of the Center for Effective Organizations at the University of Southern California. He believes that "organizations need to structure themselves around small business units that can stay in touch with the economic realities of what they are doing." By doing this, workers are given "a sense of feedback and involvement and the work environment operates as a control force, not the supervisors. It increases the value added by workers at the lowest level." Lawler further believes that teams should be allowed to develop their own business agendas, a self-management potential that business has begun to tap. Lawler adds, "Business needs more worker teams [who] do their own inventory, deal directly with customers, do their own maintenance, and can hire or fire, and decide on replacements for departing workers." [1]

Striving for Optimal Levels of Performance, Motivation, and Commitment

If you think that ideal supervisory management should be concerned only with performance, your sights are set too low. Ideal supervisory management always strives for optimal levels of performance, motivation, and commitment.

You must strive to obtain optimal performance from each employee. An optimal performance means that the employee's efforts must be of the highest quality and must be completed in a timely and efficient manner. A great job that exceeds time expectations cannot be considered an optimal performance. The tax preparer who does a top-notch job preparing your taxes but finishes your return after the April 15 deadline is not going to make you very happy. You have a penalty to deal with. Or consider the community social service agency that submits excellent proposals to deal with drug problems *after* the deadline. How many substance abusers will they reach out and help then?

Optimal supervisory management also includes optimal levels of motivation and commitment. Why are motivation and commitment so important? Employees cannot function at an optimal level unless they are motivated and self-driven to do the job. Many employees have skills that are used only when someone is standing over them. Motivated employees perform at an optimal level even when no one is standing over them. They are self-driven and take personal pride in completing tasks in a timely and qualitative manner. A manager who succeeds at encouraging optimal levels of motivation has employees who are not only skilled and highly motivated but also who can always be counted on to come through.

The remaining component of ideal supervisory management is commitment—maintaining the commitment of each person being supervised. Let's face it—once employees have the skills and motivation that you are seeking, you don't want to lose them. You need to strive to provide supervision that encourages their continued loyalty and commitment to the organization. You want them to have a sense of ownership in the organization and a commitment to staying.

A DEFINITION FOR ALL COMPONENTS

What is the definition of *Ideal Supervisory Management?* The following captures the key factors that need to be considered:

> Supervisory Management is the ongoing process and approach managers use to gain optimal levels of individual and team performance, motivation, and commitment from each person that they supervise.

The definition provides a clear focus for a manager dedicated to ideal supervisory management. It focuses on both individual and team development and it is concerned with generating optimal levels of *performance, motivation,* and *commitment* from each person. With this definition in hand, managers can be asked questions of great importance. What are the goals of supervisory management? How do you make the vision of ideal supervisory management a reality?

SIX GOALS OF SUPERVISORY MANAGEMENT

Like strategic planners, supervisory managers need to know where they are going before they can figure how to get there. They need to know what they are responsible for before they can attempt to fulfill that responsibility. This applies to managers and employees alike.

All modern industries—service, manufacturing, or farming—are similar. Each recognizes the need to train the people who produce their product or service. Employees are painstakingly told what they need to do and how to do it.

Too bad the same doesn't hold true for the managers in these industries. Yes, they're told what employees need to do. Unfortunately, the directions usually stop there. Organizations spend very little time training managers and helping them learn the skills needed to effectively manage employees. The belief is that people who become managers are born with a management instinct and are effective with little or no training.

Of course not all new managers are equally inexperienced in supervision skills. Many factors, including life experience, education, and personality, affect a person's ability to be an effective manager. The talent for managing people comes more naturally to some people than to others. While modern industry certainly puts a lot of emphasis on reinforcing the ultimate service or product goals, even innately talented managers are often given little knowledge of what managers' goals should be with each of the employees that they supervise.

Not long ago I talked with an articulate young woman who was promoted to midmanager at one of the nation's largest insurance companies. She is committed to her company and committed to excellence in every aspect of her job. She commented on some of the surprises she received in her new position.

> One of the things that I found most surprising was how little attention was paid to teaching me how to more effectively work with my staff. The goals of my department were clear. The goals of my staff were clear. The goals of the company were clear. What wasn't clear was my goals as a manager with my staff. What does a good manager do when she supervises her staff? If I know what good supervisory goals are, I'd know how to focus my attention and efforts on them.

Employees have goals in their jobs. Departments have goals. Organizations have goals. If the employee, the department, or the organization as a whole knows what their goals are, they will be in a much better position to do what is needed to achieve those goals. As a manager of staff, the same thing should be true for you. While you certainly have work goals for your department or unit, you also have management goals or responsibilities.

1. Delegation and coordination
2. Training
3. Feedback
4. Encouragement and support
5. Opportunities to learn and grow
6. Individual support and recognition

Delegation and Coordination

As management systems of the 1990s and beyond become more open and participatory, you may be wondering if managers still need to be concerned about delegating, coordinating, and directing staff. The answer is an emphatic yes. As the manager of a team of employees, you have the sole responsibility to supervise, monitor, and ensure that the work is getting done in a timely and qualitative manner.

Each member of your staff must know what is expected, how the work is to be done, when it is due, where it is to be done, and anything else related to the task or job itself. As a manager you have at the very least position power, which gives you the responsibility to delegate tasks and to ensure that the work is getting done.

Does this mean that you need to become a "tough guy" boss with a condescending attitude towards employees? Of course not. It means that you must help each of your employees understand what needs to be done and how to do it. Your challenge is to do this in a way that each employee clearly understands what is expected.

Bernard Bass, professor at the State University of New York, is an expert on leadership who believes that certain traits set exceptional managers apart: "They make themselves available to discuss particular problems, talk about career plans, review the resources the subordinate needs, critique meetings that both have been to, and go over problems the subordinate may have with his or her subordinate." [2]

In discussing delegation and coordination, you also need to remember that most managers work with a team of employees. One type of team is the "independent employee teams," in which employees' tasks are either so similar or independent that the employee requires little or no coordination with other members of the team. Another type of team is the "interdependent employee team," in which team members work closely with their colleagues because the tasks require a great deal of interdependence.

The manager's primary focus on independent employee teams is to ensure that each employee knows what he or she must do and to ensure that they complete their individual tasks in a qualitative manner and within predefined time lines.

The responsibilities of managers with interdependent employee teams are more complex. In addition to the responsibilities of the independent employee team manager, managers on interdependent employee teams must effectively delegate responsibilities and ensure the efficient and smooth coordination of services among the employees on the team.

The manager of the interdependent employee team puts much more emphasis on helping employees understand their responsibility for completing the task and for ensuring that they cooperate with other members of the team. The success or failure of the team depends on this cooperation.

Problems of power. Unfortunately, some managers on both kinds of teams have problems with the goal of delegating responsibilities effectively and ensuring coordination among team employees. In particular, they have a problem with the power that goes with their position. Two types of power problems tend to emerge.

The first concerns managers who are caught up with power. These managers think of themselves as generals in charge of the troops. They are consumed with the power of the position and they view employees as lowly troops whom they can boss around. A manager once told me, "I'm in charge. My job is to tell them what to do. I'm the boss and I pay them to work. If they don't do the job the way I tell them, they can hit the road." Those of you who have never worked for anyone like that can be grateful.

The second type of problem is with the manager who is afraid of the power. Unlike the previous manager, this manager tries not to exert power. Sometimes these managers are unsure of their roles and don't know how to deal with employees. At other times they become overly participatory. They don't provide enough direction or their directions lack clarity, and they often involve too many people—sometimes the entire team—in all decision making.

The first type of manager can cause employees to become angry because they are not respected and have little or no influence over what is happening in their work life. Employees who work for the second type of manager become frustrated over the lack of clarity or direction. "We seemed to be spinning our wheels," is a common response.

Managers must strike a proper balance by providing enough clarity and direction so that employees know what is expected of them while allowing enough leeway so that employees feel comfortable in seeking advice and asking questions.

Too much intensity and control can anger your staff. Too little direction results in staff who are uncertain of their responsibilities. Frustration often sets in. Fortunately, as you begin to learn the Functional Management Model, you will learn how to best approach each member of your staff and why specific supervisory approaches are most appropriate for specific employees.

The key thing to remember at this stage, however, is that you, as a manager, must recognize and be committed to the goal of assigning and delegating resonsibilities and providing efficient coordination among your employees.

Training and Compentency Assurance

You cannot expect your employees to do the job that they have been hired to do unless they have the skills and knowledge to do the job right. Doing the job right also means doing it within the expected timelines.

If your staff are to be held accountable for the work that they are doing, they must receive the necessary training to do the job in the manner that you expect. It is not fair to hold employees accountable for the successful completion of tasks they weren't adequately trained to do.

You are not expected to provide the actual training. There may be some jobs you supervise that you have not been trained to do. No one can be an expert in every area. It is not expected that the president or chief executive officer knows how to do everything within the organization. The CEO of IBM may know marketing, but may not have been trained in computer technology. But managers at any level must see that their subordinates get the training that they need.

Even if you have the expertise, you may not have the time to do the training. In many health and human service fields, staff are required to learn basic first aid and CPR. Managers normally have these skills and some may even be certified to teach them. But because the training is time consuming, most managers in these fields arrange for the training of their staff.

Knowing the skill level of staff is essential. The goal of ensuring that staff are trained plays a major role in the Functional Management Model. Think about it. If you have an employee who is not doing the job that you expect him or her to do, normally you ask, "Why?" Why is this person not doing the job? Or not completing it in the normally required time? Or in a quality way?

You really won't know what to do with that person until you can answer the why. For example, if you discovered the answer to be that the employee has not sufficiently learned the skills to do the job, you would immediately respond by providing the person with training. On the other hand, if you know that the person has the skills, then more training is not the answer. Something else must be done. Again, the Functional Management Model will provide you with a clear understanding of what you need to do.

Feedback

As a manager, one of your most important goals is that of providing feedback to each of your employees. Nothing is more effective and more responsive to employee development than the feedback an employee receives from the supervisor or other members of the organization.

A study was made on what type of feedback adolescents wanted most from their parents. The choices that they were given were positive feedback, negative feedback, and no feedback. Not surprisingly, most adolescents responded that they wanted to hear positive feedback. What did surprise researchers was their second choice. If they couldn't receive positive feedback, then they preferred negative feedback over no feedback at all. With negative feedback, adolescents at least felt that their parents cared enough to be involved. With no feedback, they received neither validation for good performance nor constructive criticism for mistakes. Without feedback, the implication was that parents didn't care enough to let the adolescents know how they were doing.

You are the same way. Each of you strives to do your jobs in the best way you know how. If you are honest about it, you will readily admit that you like and appreciate positive feedback. It makes you feel good about what you do and lets you know that you are appreciated.

While you may not want to receive negative feedback, you can learn from it. When you are shown how you are doing things wrong, you learn how to do things right. With no feedback, you don't get a sense that people appreciate the good things that you do.

The importance of immediate feedback. Both positive and negative feedback are important. Negative feedback—a better term is "constructive criticism"—can be extremely helpful to an employee. If you are doing something wrong, wouldn't you like your supervisor to let you know? Wouldn't you appreciate knowing that your performance is not meeting expectations so that you could correct it?

At a large training seminar for midmanagers and senior managers in Connecticut, the question was asked, "If you are doing something wrong and your supervisor is aware of it, when would you like your supervisor to tell you?" The overwhelming answer was, "Immediately."

A second question, "When you as a manager become aware that one of your employees is not performing a task in the expected way, when would you tell the employee?" brought different responses from a number of managers: "In our next supervisory session." "When we have our quarterly evaluations." "When I have the time." "When I am better prepared." There was an obvious conflict between what these managers wanted for themselves and what they were willing to provide their employees.

Finally, line staff in trainings throughout the country were asked when they would like their manager to tell them they were doing something wrong. Their answers reflect what mid- and senior managers want for themselves. "Immediately!" They felt it is critical to learn as soon as possible when they are doing something wrong. As one participant explained, "I'm committed to doing the best job possible. How can I possibly correct my mistakes if no one tells me I'm doing something wrong. What's worse is that the longer I do something wrong, the harder it will be to change." Your staff wants the same thing you want. If they are doing something wrong, they want to know immediately. They don't want to wait until their next supervisory session with you.

Feedback is important. It validates good performance and helps a staff person correct faulty performance. Given in a positive and appropriate way, feedback can help build trust between you and your employees. It is also the best way to ensure that employees know how to provide services that meet the expectations of the organization.

Encouragement and Support

Encouragement and support are one type of feedback. It is positive feedback directed at promoting and strengthening positive performance while also enhancing an employee's sense of security and self-esteem in the workplace. It is a form of feedback that tells employees that they have management support in their work-specific efforts.

The encouragement and support of staff are important goals for managers. It is one of the most effective ways of letting employees know that the manager is aware of their efforts, and appreciates and supports them. Unfortunately, it is a goal that most managers don't recognize or don't utilize often enough.

It means a great deal. The need for employees to feel encouragement and support from their superiors is not limited to line staff. I went to Ohio to provide executive-level training for the presidents and CEOs of some of the state's largest mental health centers. They managed some very challenging and complex organizations, worked long hours, and, for the most part, did an excellent job serving the needs of the mentally ill and their families.

Following the formal training, an informal executive session was held only with the CEOs. One discussion question centered on what would make their job more satisfying. One member stated, "It would sure be nice if our boards were more aware of what was going on and provided us with a little more positive feedback, encouragement, and support. Sometimes, I feel like no one really appreciates all that I am going through." This sentiment was shared by other members of the session.

At later meetings, I learned that the feelings expressed in Ohio were shared by leaders in a wide variety of fields. It is sometimes not easy to admit, but all managers appreciate receiving recognition for their work or encouragement and support for the many challenges that they face.

If leaders of organizations value encouragement and support, it makes sense that employees would value them too. The executives in Ohio looked to people who were overseeing their work—in many cases the board of directors. The person who most closely oversees your employee's work is *you*. You are in the best position to provide your employees with encouragement and support.

Encouragement and support are not only appreciated when they come from the boss or from someone else who oversees your work, but also when they come from colleagues. Your coworkers know what you are doing and see the challenges that you face. Managers, too, like hearing words of appreciation from their staff. The best organizations to work for are those in which staff at all levels recognize and express appreciation and support for each other.

This is not a one-way street. It works up, down, and sideways. We all have the responsibility to let the people we work with—employees, colleagues and bosses—know that we appreciate what they've done. Good managers know that it makes staff feel better about themselves, better about their work, and better about their organization. It is a simple management tool that encourages motivation and commitment by staff.

Opportunities to Learn and Grow

As employees mature in their jobs, they often evolve to the point where they have learned all that there is about the job. These employees often become bored and look for other options. To renew inspiration in these high-performing employees, you must provide them with opportunities to learn new skills and to enhance their personal and professional growth. There is a certain amount of excitement associated with learning new skills and in growing as a person and as a professional.

The good side of this situation is that the job itself is less threatening to the employee. He or she knows that they can do it and have proved it. The bad side is that now the job has become less challenging and is no longer exciting.

An approach to motivation.   Frederick Herzberg is a well-known motivational theorist who has conducted extensive research on what motivates people. Herzberg's major contribution is called motivational-hygeine theory.[3]

In his research Herzberg found that there were a number of trinsic and intrinsic factors associated with work. Some of those factors motivated people when they were present. He was surprised to discover, however, that there were other factors that did not motivate people when they were present, but caused employees to feel demotivated when they were *not* present. For example, if company policies were administered in an uneven manner, employees tended to become demoralized and demotivated. If company policies were good and administered in a fair and reasonable manner, employees felt good but weren't more motivated because of that. It appeared that if, as part of their jobs, employees expected certain things, the presence of these things—like good policies that were administered fairly—were not likely to re-energize and motivate them.

Herzberg did find, however, that employees were motivated when their managers provided them with opportunities to learn new skills, to grow personally and professionally, and to be challenged. Learning new skills and doing something that helps you grow personally and professionally is a challenge and provides a sense of satisfaction.

An example may be found by reflecting on the beginning of your career. You were constantly acquiring new knowledge and skills, being challenged, and growing as a professional. A personnel recruiter in an insurance company once told me, "Everything was new. Every day I was learning new skills. Every night I went home excited about what I had learned and looked forward to meeting the challenges of the next day."

As a manager, your challenge is to find ways to motivate your staff, particularly your higher performing staff. You need to know when to provide activities that encourage learning and growth and how to do so effectively. In this way, a successful manager will keep the commitment and enthusiasm of staff.

How challenges motivate staff.   People don't like to be bored. They want to use their skills and expertise. When asked if

they would prefer a job that challenges them or one that is predictable, the vast majority of respondents at our training sessions
preferred jobs that challenge their skills and expertise. This
doesn't mean that people want to be in life-or-death situations.
They don't want their job to be one where at every turn they face a
challenge with a high probability of failure.

Challenging experiences provide employees with the opportunity to feel excited about what they are are doing and to feel good
and fulfilled about their successes. Is this really true? Let's test it
out with you.

Does it make sense for you?   Think of a time during your
working career when your work excited and challenged you. Try
to remember all of the things that were going on during that time.
Who was your supervisor? Who were you working with? What
were you doing? How long did it last? What made this time so
exciting and so special? Why was it an experience that you were
glad that you had?

Like most people, you probably had little trouble remembering
an experience that was exciting and fulfilling, one that challenged
your skills and creativity. I have been fortunate to have had a
number of such experiences. One, for example, concerned a "future study" on changes affecting the workforce in the mental
health field. It required identifying the top 100 mental health
experts in the country, tracking them down, and conducting wide-
ranging interviews with them. It also required a comprehensive
analysis, the identification of major trends, and the development of a set of concise recommendations for leaders in the
mental health field to consider as they planned for the future.
The effort was difficult, yet exciting. It required the use of all
my skills and the learning of new ones. It was a challenging
experience that provided me with the opportunity to learn and
grow.

As a manager, one critical goal is to seek out opportunities for
your employees to continue to grow. You must find a way to
provide such an experience within the boundaries of their job. It
might mean asking a particular employee to develop a new procedures manual, to act as a mentor to a new employee, or—with the
right skills—resolve a particular problem in the workplace. What-

ever the task, your goal is to provide them with a challenge that they can achieve and at the same time is exciting.

Providing employees with challenging opportunities and the opportunities to grow are usually more appropriate for higher functioning employees who have proved themselves and have mastered all of the skills associated with the job. You need to determine which employees are most appropriate for this goal and how you can best implement it. These and other questions will be answered as you get into the Functional Management Model.

Individual Support and Recognition

The first four supervisory management goals are job-specific. They call on the manager to provide a range of behaviors or efforts directed at strengthening an employee's functioning on the job itself. The fifth and sixth goals are directed at finding ways to make the overall work experience more supportive and responsive to the individual needs of each employee.

This is accomplished through the two types of individual support and recognition efforts that you are responsible for achieving: structural enhancement and personal enhancement. The former are structured into your employees' work environment; the latter you control and can personalize in response to the individual needs of each employee. Both are called *enhancers* because they increase the level of the organization's response to its employees, increase employee recognition and appreciation for the organization, and heighten the employee potential of staying with the organization.

Structural enhancers. Most organizations throughout the world have adopted enhancement as a means to keep employees motivated and committed to continuing their employment with the organization. Structural enhancement efforts are normally tied to longevity. They include pay, benefits, vacation time, pension, term rewards, and other incentives designed to reward employees for their continued commitment.

Everyone has experienced enhancers. The longer you stay at a specific organization, the more enhancers you are eligible to receive. For example, you stay one year, meet the expectations of the job, and you get a raise. Stay two years and you get an extra week of vacation or become eligible for the organization's pension. Stay five years and you receive a cash bonus, a gift, or other type of tangible reward.

While not all organizations have the same kinds of structural enhancers, most do have some form of them. While you, as a manager, normally have little control over these, you do have the responsibility to ensure that your employees receive everything for which they are eligible. In talking with employees about their jobs and compensation, you must let them know what you think is unique or special about your organization's enhancers. A manager in a large state agency in Massachusetts said that while there were many limitations to working for state government, there were also a few enhancers that the staff greatly appreciated, such as the state's pension program. "You would be surprised how the state's pension system keeps many employees motivated and committed to their jobs."

As a manager, you have the responsibility to see that your employees are aware of the organization's structural enhancers and receive everything for which they are eligible and when they are due. One manager at an automobile plant writes her employees a short note letting them know what changes are coming up and congratulates them on becoming eligible. It is a nice touch that lets her staff know that she is on top of things and concerned for their welfare.

Personal enhancers. Personal enhancers are enhancers that managers *can* do something about. They are things that you do to make the workplace more personally supportive and personally responsive to the individual needs of your employees.

Examples range from allowing a high-functioning employee the opportunity to participate on a task force, to establishing flextime for employees, to starting a support group for staff who share a similar need. One organization created a task force to explore programs to help employees kick smoking and arranged to have the program in the organization's conference room. Another group started a weight-loss program, while a third started a single-parent support group.

Some organizations have negotiated with local health clubs and arranged for employee discounts. Others have found that employees appreciated being told what was going on in the organization and scheduled a one-hour brunch once a month to update people and to encourage socializing. One organization discovered that a number of its employees were interested in participating on community task forces, so it made arrangements for employees to work with these groups both during work hours and on their own time. Another organization allowed its higher functioning staff to participate on committees that were planning future efforts and projects for the organization. Yet another organization expanded the responsibilities and authority of higher functioning employees.

In some ways, it really doesn't matter what kind of personal enhancer you use with a specific employee. What matters is that you come up with ideas that respond to the personal needs of your employees, particularly the higher functioning ones.

Personal enhancers are a very effective means of keeping higher functioning employees motivated and excited about their jobs. Because goals five and six—opportunities to learn and grow, and individual support and recognition—are so important to your higher functioning employees and essential to the Functional Management Model, some effective ways for achieving these goals will be provided in chapter 3.

The Importance of the Six Goals

All six goals respond to specific needs of employees. They are not abstract or theoretical concepts. They provide a blueprint that defines the various responsibilities or challenges you face as a manager. The challenge is to know when one goal might be more appropriate for a specific employee than another. Employees certainly do not all have the same needs at the same time. The employee who is with the organization for two weeks will obviously have a different set of needs than the employee who has been with the organization for years. Even more important is the need to know what behaviors or efforts you need to exhibit or use in order to achieve each of the goals.

CREATING A TONE FOR
OPTIMAL SUPERVISION

The ultimate goal in supervision is to ensure maximum levels of performance, motivation, and commitment by each of the employees that you supervise. The six goals do not address management approach to supervision. How should you treat the people you supervise? What tone should you set?

In the late 1950s Douglas McGregor, the noted organizational theorist, conducted extensive studies on how supervisors' assumptions affected the motivation of staff. McGregor identified two extremes of supervisors. One worked under the assumption that employees were inherently lazy, didn't like to work, had little motivation, and needed to be closely controlled and monitored. He called this assumption of human nature Theory X.

The opposite kind of supervisor is much more positive about human nature. This supervisor views employees as being willing to work. This supervisor sees that employees have creative potential, could be self-directed and self-motivated if properly supported, and are willing to learn and be committed to the goals of the organization. McGregor called this assumption Theory Y.[4]

Normally managers are not at one end or the other of this spectrum. What is important to note is that in the late 1950s and early 60s, McGregor found that those managers who believed more in Theory Y tended to have staff who were more highly motivated and more committed to the goals and efforts of their organization.

Encouraging Employee Growth and Involvement

Twenty years later, in what may have been the all-time best-seller in the history of modern management, *In Search of Excellence*, Tom Peters and Bob Waterman outlined eight major attributes that they tended to find consistently in exceptional companies. One of the key attributes they termed "productivity through people." They pointed out that the organizations that tended to thrive were those which respected their employees, established an environment of trust, and constantly recognized that employees were the real key to productivity.

Peters and Waterman's position was clear. "Treat people as adults. Treat them as partners; treat them with dignity; treat them with respect. Treat them—not capital spending or automation—as the primary source of productivity gains. These are the fundamental lessons from the excellent companies research."[5]

An equally compelling perspective is provided by James Kinnear, former president and CEO of Texaco. Asked how important he believed it was for managers to encourage the professional development of their employees, Kinnear responded:

> It is vital. The success of any company depends, in the final analysis, on the superiority of its human talent, and the skill with which that talent is developed and used. A company can have excellent franchises, market shares, plant and equipment. But human talent is required to translate those assets into today's profits. And tomorrow's success will be built on ideas, innovation and vision—qualities that only human beings can produce. A company that fails to listen to those ideas or encourage the full development of its human talent is wasting precious resources and losing competitive ground to companies that do. It is imperative that the CEO make sure that his/her managers understand that, among their prime responsibilities, is encouraging and developing employees, and listening to them.[6]

Leaders of organizations other than large national or multinational organizations also feel that way about their employees. Diana Buckley, executive director of Parents and Children Together, a Honolulu-based child service agency, puts tremendous emphasis on respecting and supporting employees. "There is no greater responsibility a supervisor has than supporting her or his staff," she says. "Staff are the heart and soul of an organization. It is their success or failure that will make the greatest difference in the lives of the children and families we serve. Our goal must always be to support, respect, and encourage the growth of each member of our staff."[7]

Supervisory Excellence and Total Quality Management

What are we finding as we move through the 1990s toward the 21st century? We find that the emphasis on respecting, empowering, and involving employees is one of the centerpieces of total quality management, the newest wave of management philosophy. Led by management gurus, Philip Crosby, W. Edward Deming, A. Feigenbaum, and Juran Juran,[8] American management has begun to move seriously toward improving quality under the flag of total quality management. Each of these writers has developed excellent strategies for managers to achieve total quality, zero defects, and other means to improve quality.

The theorists share a number of firm beliefs: that modern organizations must make a total commitment to providing exceptional quality, that a total commitment must be made to continuous improvement in quality, and that every level, position, and employee must be involved in total quality management.

What does all this have to do with supervisory management? Who is going to make quality a reality? While consultants and senior managers might be doing everything they can to model a commitment to total quality, it's the supervisors and midmanagers who will make total quality a reality and who must be relied on to responsibly support, encourage, and empower the workers of the organization. If they are unsuccessful and workers do not feel supported and empowered, your organization's products and services will suffer.

Jerry Bowles and Joshua Hammond studied 50 companies heavily involved in the total quality movement. Their research led to an interesting finding, "A profound lesson of the quality movement is that worker satisfaction is inseparable from customer satisfaction."[9]

The point of all this is simple. What was true in the past and true today will be more true than ever in the years ahead. Employee involvement, commitment, motivation, and satisfaction are the cornerstones of total quality management efforts and are clearly essential to the success of organizations.

Optimal supervisory management is the means to make this happen. And the best way to achieve optimal supervisory management is by treating each of your employees as an adult who can be respected and trusted. That's how you would want to be treated and that's how your employees want to be treated. The tone you set will dramatically affect your ability to supervise, motivate, and gain maximum levels of performance and commitment from your employees. It will also help you achieve the six supervisory goals more effectively.

Chapter Three

Supervisory Options: The Foundation for Supervision

D o you remember the first job you ever had? Maybe it was working in your local supermarket or clothing store. Ringing a register at the local drugstore. Waiting tables. Answering the phone and filing at a local office. Working as a summer camp counselor. Or any one of a thousand jobs that introduce young people to the realities of work.

For days prior to starting the job, you probably went through the same classic ritual, nervous and unsure of yourself. "Can I do it? What if . . . ? Maybe I'll change my mind." Somehow you lived through it.

And do you remember how you ultimately learned the job? When you got to work, someone—usually your boss—told you what you had to do. Then someone showed you how to do it—sometimes two, three, or even ten times. As you became more proficient, you learned some tricks to make the job easier. Finally, when you became really proficient, you were given the ultimate honor: you were allowed to show a new employee how to do it.

What is surprising about all this is that, for the most part, it worked. You learned the job. You found ways to make it easier. Your confidence grew. And you became a success.

PRESENT-DAY REALITIES OF SUPERVISORY TRAINING

Now, recall what it was like when you became a manager. Maybe you applied for the job and got it. Maybe you were promoted. Maybe you were forced into the job because you were next in line or were "the best employee available." If you were like most people, you probably felt just like you did on the first day of your first job. "Can I do it?" "What if . . . ?" "Maybe I'll change my mind." But at this point things begin to change drastically.

With a little bit of luck, you might have received orientation. You learned exciting things about forms, regulations, insurance, and policies. If you were lucky you also were probably told what your unit or department was supposed to do. You might have been told everything . . . everything except how to get your employees to effectively and enthusiastically do what has to be done.

Failures of Supervisory Management Training

Most organizations fail to provide managers with the knowledge and skills they need to be effective. They thrust the person into the role, talk about what is expected of the unit or department, and encourage him or her to get the most out of staff.

Mary was named as department head in a large retail store of a national chain. She was put in charge of 15 people. Mary was articulate and committed, and she knew what senior management expected of her department. She had received training in every aspect of her job except one—how to supervise and get the most out of her employees.

Mary failed to provide the right levels of direction and support. She alienated her higher performers. Productivity decreased. Morale went down. Turnover increased. Finally, out of frustration, Mary left the company. All this occurred because the retail store failed to teach Mary "how" to supervise.

If you became a manager without any training about gaining the most from your employees, you belong to a not-so-elite club of people who were not supported responsibly by their organization. However, it's not too late for people who have managers report to them. You can still provide them with the training and skills needed to be successful supervisory managers, and you can teach them what is necessary to achieve their supervisory goals.

HOW TO ACHIEVE YOUR SUPERVISORY MANAGEMENT GOALS

Remember that optimal supervisory management is defined as the ongoing process and approaches managers use to gain optimal levels of individual and team performance, motivation, and commitment from each person they supervise.

How do you achieve the six supervisory management goals directed at making optimal supervisory management a reality?

In many ways, the behaviors or skills needed to respond to these goals are implied in the goals themselves. These goals break down into three logical categories that suggest three specific types of behaviors by the manager.

This chapter outlines the three major supervisory behaviors needed for optimal supervisory management and the key skills most associated with each. Together, the behaviors and skills will provide you with a strong foundation for effectively using the Functional Management Model.

Each of the three behaviors addresses two specific supervisory management goals. These three key behaviors most closely associated with optimal supervisory management are directive behavior, work-specific support, and personal and professional development support.

Directive Behavior

Goals one and two—delegation and coordination and training and competency assurance—cover learning what is necessary to do the job efficiently and effectively. They are job-specific goals wherein the employee needs to learn skills related to the job. In some cases, it means simply knowing what is expected on a particular day. In others, particularly with new employees, they will need to learn a new set of skills on performing the job.

To achieve these two goals, you need to provide a great deal of direction so the behavior most called for is directive behavior. This might mean telling an employee what to do, how to do it, where to do it, when to do it, and why the job must be done that way. In other cases, directive behavior might mean arranging for an employee to receive training and learn the job skills. In still other cases, it may mean working with that employee and other employees to ensure that they are coordinating their efforts and working in harmony.

Work-Specific Support

Goals three and four of optimal supervisory management are feedback and encouragement and support. As employees learn a job, they need task-related feedback on how they are doing and how they might improve their performance. Encouragement and support provide them with a sense of being appreciated and supported by their manager and organization.

In today's highly competitive work environment, the importance of work-specific support cannot be overstated. As its name suggests, work-specific support is support of the employee in relationship to the job or particular task that the employee is doing. How you support and encourage the work of your employees translates directly into how motivated and how committed they will be to maintaining standards of performance.

Today's movement toward exceptional customer service and total quality management are built on the premise that motivated employees are essential to providing high quality services and products. In their book on customer service, *Service America*, Karl Albrecht and Ron Zemke state emphatically that "to have a high standard of service, it is necessary to create and maintain a motivating environment in which service people can find personal reasons for committing their energies to the benefit of the customer."[1]

Work-specific support ensures that employees always know how they are doing and what they can do to improve. It helps employees feel good about what they are doing. Work-specific support is one of the best ways for a manager to motivate an employee toward achieving a high performance level.

Personal and Professional Development Support

The manager who focuses only on the present efforts of employees is making a mistake. Employees normally want to do a good job in their present tasks, but they also want to be challenged in their work, to learn and grow professionally, and to feel that their individual needs are supported by the organization. Employees also want to feel good about where they work.

Kaoru Ishikawa, president of the Musashi Institute of Technology in Japan, is acknowledged as one of the most sought-after gurus of the total quality management movement. Companies throughout the world, including IBM and Ford, have been guided by his principles.

Ishikawa is very clear on how responsible managers are for ensuring the happiness, satisfaction, and commitment of the staff. Ishikawa argues that "the first concern of the company is the happiness of people who are connected with it. If the people do not feel happy and cannot be made to feel happy, that company does not deserve to exist."[2]

You, as a manager, must initiate efforts to provide each of your employees with the opportunities to grow personally and professionally, and to recognize and respond to their individual needs. You must do what you can to help create a work environment that is positive, motivating, and responsive to the individual and collective needs of your employees. Your behavior in this respect is called personal and professional development support. It addresses goals five and six—opportunities to learn and grow and individual support and recognition.

Personal and professional development support focuses on the individual, not the job, and is designed to help employees improve themselves personally and professionally. These efforts are not totally divorced from the job, but they are initiated chiefly to improve a person's capacities or to make the work environment more supportive and responsive to his or her personal and professional needs.

When you send employees to training on conflict management, what they learn will help them on the job. But it will also help them in future jobs and could assist them in their personal lives. In some ways, the old adage is true. You can kill two birds with one stone—or one training program.

For a better understanding of the relationship between the three behaviors—directive behavior, work-specific support, and personal and professional development support—and the six goals of supervisory management, see the depiction of their interrelationship on p. 93. Note that each of the behaviors is designed to respond to two of the specific goals. As a manager, you cannot avoid being responsible for all six goals. But by using all three behaviors, appropriately, you place yourself in the best possible position to effectively achieve all six goals, and you are taking a great step toward achieving optimal supervisory management.

Effects of Optimal Supervisory Management

When you are supervising and managing your staff effectively, achieving all six goals, and using the supervisory management behaviors effectively, your staff know it and you know it.

Staff feel recognized and supported. They feel that they are getting the right training and right direction to do the job right. They feel that their efforts are effectively coordinated with colleagues and others. They know their roles and responsibilities and those of others.

They also feel that they are getting timely and on-going positive feedback on their work. They know that their manager is fair, so they are receptive to receiving constructive feedback that helps them succeed on the job.

Finally, employees know that their manager is concerned with more than the day-to-day realities of work. The manager's actions, behaviors, and efforts show concern about their personal and professional development. They know that their manager will work with them in addressing personal issues that affect their job performance.

And what do you—as a manager—see? You see staff who are happy and committed to their jobs and to the organization. They are highly motivated and want to succeed. They come across as feeling good about themselves and good about what they do. Performance, morale, and overall satisfaction are high.

SUCCESSFULLY USING THE THREE MANAGEMENT BEHAVIORS

Strong performance, motivation, morale, and commitment by employees don't just happen. They come about because you, the manager, effectively use the three behaviors, not simply know what the three behaviors are.

It sounds easy, doesn't it? Who doesn't know how to give good direction? Who would be confused about how to give good work-specific support? What manager isn't aware of how to identify and respond to the personal needs of employees? And who isn't committed to helping employees grow and develop professionally? Most of us know a great deal about each of these areas but tend to forget them as we deal with the reality of work. Nevertheless, because each of these behaviors is essential to effective supervision and use of the Functional Management Model, it is important to outline key rules on how to use each behavior.

Learning from Reality

Thousands of people have been trained in the Functional Management Model. In the workshops or seminars, participants are broken into groups. Each group is asked to develop a list of recommendations in response to one of five questions. All five questions are always asked and each group responds to only one.

1. What do effective managers do in order to give effective directions?
2. What do ineffective managers do when they give poor directions?
3. What should managers do in order to give effective work-specific support?
4. What are all the things that managers can do to improve the quality of work life of their organization or to respond to the appropriate personal needs of staff?
5. What are all the things that managers can do to support the professional development of the staff?

Question two is really the flip side of question one, but it is asked so that directive behaviors can be viewed from a different perspective and to ensure a broad response. Questions four and five divide personal and professional development support into two distinct categories of behaviors. This helps to ensure that the personal and professional needs of employees are thoroughly analyzed. The responses provide an invaluable set of recommendations for the most effective use of all three categories of behaviors.

Why Focus on the Three Supervisory Behaviors?

The three supervisory management behaviors represent the core skills that you need to learn to be an effective supervisory manager. Learn these skills and you dramatically improve your ability to effectively supervise, motivate, and gain optimal levels of performance and commitment from your employees. The three behaviors are not specific to the Functional Management Model. However, the skills associated with these behaviors are at the core of most contemporary management models and are certainly the core skills learned by effective managers.

Like many managers, you are probably saying, "Give me a break. At this stage in my career, I certainly know how to give people direction and how to support them on the job. I also know how to respond to their needs for personal and professional development."

You probably do know how to do these things, but that's not what matters. The real issue is not what you know, but what you do with what you know. You could be the most knowledgeable manager in the world, but if you don't use what you know, what good is it?

John had recently graduated with honors from an MBA program at a state university. He was obviously intelligent and was excelling in the technical aspects of his job. Unfortunately, he was failing miserably as a supervisor. He was so anxious to succeed on the job that he paid little attention to supervising his employees. He was putting all his energies into the technical aspects of his job and little or no energy into the supervisory aspects.

When I met John, he was obviously frustrated and discouraged. As we talked, it became clear that he knew what to do. He had the knowledge. Knew human relations theory. He even recalled writing papers on gaining employee motivation and improving employee morale. The only thing he failed to do was to apply what he learned.

I don't want this to happen to you. To ensure that you have the knowledge to be an effective supervisor, I am asking you to consider the three supervisory management skills from two perspectives.

First, you must have a clear understanding of how to use the three skills. Brief recommendations will be presented on how to effectively use each of the skills. The recommendations combine the input and real-life experience of thousands of managers, who were workshop participants, with findings from contemporary management research and practice. While not exhaustive, they represent consistently recommended responses.

Second, to be a truly effective manager, you need more than knowledge. You need to implement what you know. The brief Management Plus Supervisory Effectiveness Survey questionnaire (see Chart 3.2) asks you to rate yourself on a number of variables.

PROVIDING DIRECTIVE BEHAVIOR

As outlined earlier, directive behaviors are behaviors you initiate to let employees know what they need to do, how and when to do it, and an array of other expectations geared to improving their skills and job performance. Six recommendations for providing clear directive behavior stand out.

Be specific.   Avoid using vague or ambiguous terms when providing direction. Don't say, "I want you to be more responsive to our customers." What does this mean? What should the employee do to be more responsive? Be specific. "I'd like you to greet customers within two minutes of their entering the store. Ask them how you can help. If you learn their name, use it." The more specific you are, the clearer your expectations are to the employee.

Ask employees to state in their own words their understanding of what you expect.   It doesn't matter what you say when giving direction as long as your employees understand what you said. One way to ensure that you are in complete agreement is to ask them to repeat to you what their understanding is. In this way, you reinforce to the employee the importance of their understanding your directions or expectations clearly. You in turn are able to clarify any misunderstandings quickly.

Explain how your directions fit into the big picture. For many employees, learning a new task is made easier when they see how it fits into the big picture. Your explanation of the relation to the whole of what employees learn does two things. First, it gives employees a context for understanding what they are doing. Second, by demonstrating that the whole is dependent on their effort, you reinforce the importance of their work.

Tailor training and directives to the competency level of the employee. Nothing frustrates employees more than being regarded as having less knowledge and fewer skills than they actually have. From the beginning, you should strive to determine an employee's knowledge and skills; then train and instruct the employee based on his or her present status. If an employee already knows a specific skill, it is frustrating to both the employee and yourself to reeducate that employee.

Provide time lines and parameters for all efforts. During training or giving of directions, employees must understand the scope of their responsibility and authority. They should know what you expect and how and when you expect it. This also applies to ongoing efforts; complex directives should be put in writing.

It does not help an employee to say, "I want a quality job done on this project and I want it done in a timely way." Instead you define specifically what you expect. If you want a written report by Tuesday at five o'clock, simply say, "I want a written report on this by Tuesday at 5:00."

Monitor and follow-up. When you initially become involved with an employee, what you tell him or her is important because you said it is important. If you do not set up the mechanisms to monitor and follow up on your directives, employees quickly begin asking themselves, "Is it really that important?" But if you monitor and follow up on their performance in a particular area, they'll quickly know the answer. Let's face it. If you know your boss is monitoring specific aspects of your performance, don't you tend to pay more attention to these areas?

These are not the only rules for providing optimal direction. Others could certainly be added. What these rules do, however, is provide a strong set of standards for ensuring that your directives are effective and clearly understood.

PROVIDING WORK-SPECIFIC SUPPORT

Work-specific support concerns support of the employee on the task itself. It is not blind positive support. It is honest support that may correct an employee's performance but which is always done in a positive manner.

Participants in the sessions throughout the country identified a broad range of work-specific supportive efforts that they have used effectively. The following five have been consistently identified.

Hold regularly scheduled supervisory meetings. Provide your employees with predictable times when they can meet with you. These sessions allow employees the opportunity to talk about what they did and to get your feedback. Problems can be talked through. Strategies can be developed. New skills can be trained. Employees can be corrected and supported at the same time. What you do in these sessions depends on what you feel would be most helpful to the employee. One of the most effective ways that you can support your employees is suggested by Sidney Simon, professor at the University of Massachusetts, and a leader in the field of values clarification. Simon says that a manager should say three things to his or her employee.

1. What did you do?
2. How did it go?
3. What can I do to help?

I would add a fourth. "What would you do differently to make things go even more smoothly?" These four questions provide employees with the opportunity to reflect on their performance and think through how they could have made things go more effectively. Best of all, when you ask, "What can I do to help?" you make it clear to the employee that you are truly supportive and committed to their development.

Provide feedback as soon as possible after an event. People learn best when they receive feedback soon after completing the effort. Why is bowling America's number one participant sport? One reason is because the bowler gets immediate feedback on his or her performance. Within seconds of bowling the ball, they receive either positive feedback for knocking down pins or negative feedback for not knocking down enough. In the workplace, the closer the feedback is to a person's exhibiting a certain behavior, the more helpful it will be.

Ensure that ongoing support is readily available. The open door policy, immediate availability of resources, administrative support, and appropriate tools can be made available by managers to their employees in support of their work-specific efforts. The more employees know that resources and tools are immediately available, the more supported and the more confident they will feel about their efforts.

Utilize the 80/20 Rule when supporting your staff. The 80/20 Rule is simple: 80 percent of the time you should give your staff positive feedback, encouragement, and support; you should focus on negative things no more than 20 percent of the time. This rule makes a lot of sense. In most cases, your employees do good work, probably far more than 80 percent of the time. Positive feedback encourages and reinforces positive performance.

Unfortunately, managers tend to respond more to negative than to positive actions. The 80/20 Rule is a strong reminder that the managerial focus should always be on supporting and encouraging positive performance rather than looking for problems. If you say that an employee deserves negative feedback, then the obvious question is, "Why do you keep this employee?"

Model what you expect from your employees. How you function on the job is more important than what you say. Have you ever seen a manager who talks a good game but in practice is a nonsupportive manager?

Bill was a supervisor in a manufacturing plant. Although young, he was ambitious and reliable, and had moved up in the organization. In an effort to improve himself, he signed up for a management course at a local junior college, only to find that the instructor was his immediate supervisor. The course surprised Bill in two ways. First, he was surprised by how much theoretical knowledge the supervisor knew. Second, he was depressed by the realization that his supervisor—the instructor—never practiced what he preached.

Staff look to you as their supervisor and rate your behavior far more than your rhetoric. Work with your employees. Go out of your way to exhibit the kind of behavior you expect from your employees. This encourages similar types of behaviors among your employees.

Together, these five suggestions provide employees with a clear sense of what is expected of them. It also provides them with a strong sense that their work-specific efforts are being monitored, encouraged, and supported.

PROVIDING PERSONAL AND PROFESSIONAL DEVELOPMENT SUPPORT

The third major skill exceptional managers must be able to utilize are skills and efforts directed at responding to the personal needs and improving the professional capacity of their employees. Managers must strive to develop a work environment that is positive and supportive to the personal and professional development of each of the employees.

Max DePree is the chairman and CEO of Herman Miller, Inc., a nationally known furniture maker. *Fortune* magazine named De-Pree's company as one of the 10 best managed and most innovative companies in the country. Herman Miller was also chosen as one of the 100 best companies in the United States to work for. And it was one of the top 15 companies in terms of ambiance, those qualities that affect personal and professional development and the quality of work life of employees.[3]

DePree feels strongly that leaders must develop a work environment that is conducive to high-quality work and high-quality relationships. In his book, *Leadership Is an Art*, DePree writes, "Leaders need to foster environments and work processes within which people can develop high-quality relationships—relationships with each other, relationships with the group with which we work, relationships with our clients and customers."[4] Fostering this type of positive environment and responding to the personal and professional needs of employees are two clear considerations in personal and professional development support.

Personal and professional development support differs in a fundamental way from directive behavior and work-specific support. The latter are more general in nature; they are applied basically the same way to all industries. Personal and professional development behaviors, however, are more organization-specific, meaning that their application must be done within the context of each industry. What works for IBM or General Motors may not be appropriate in a city hospital, a state agency, or a small retail store. Your challenge as a manager is to clearly understand the realities of your organization and to develop strategies that work within those realities.

To simplify this, I have separated personal development support from professional development support. This allows you to have a much better understanding of how to apply both components of this third supervisory behavior.

Responding to the Personal Needs of Staff

To respond to the personal needs of your staff, there are two ways you can approach this challenge. First, you can focus on improving the quality of worklife of *everyone* on your team. Second, you can individualize the response to the unique needs of each employee. Who is the single person with the best knowledge of the personal needs of specific employees?

In terms of the overall quality of work life, can you institute flex time? Hold regular staff meetings? Have parties for special occasions? Invite staff to planning retreats? Have regular team meetings? Start support groups?

The second approach is more focused. Use your insights and experience with each staff member to try to come up with the best ways to respond to their specific needs. By making available opportunities that respond to the individual needs of employees, you are sending a message: we care about you and we value your efforts. We are trying to find ways to make your work life more satisfying and more responsive to your personal needs.

Your knowledge and instincts may work in responding to the personal needs of each of your employees, but in my experience, it is not the best way to identify the best response. Take a second and more direct approach. Ask the employees.

They obviously have the best sense of a good response to their personal needs. They know what would make the quality of *their* work life better.

Your initial reaction as a manager may be that the employees will ask for the world and you won't be able to respond. Don't sell your employees short. At the sessions with organizations throughout the country, participants are asked the following question:

> Given all the realities you know about the resources and limitations of your organization, what are all the things it could do to respond to your personal needs and improve your quality of work life?

Participants never came up with less than three ideas. Most came up with seven or more. Rarely were they unrealistic, overdemanding, or centered solely on more money.

> In a session with CPAs and auditors of a very large organization, the average number of responses per individual was five with a low of three and a high of eleven. The financial people looked for a number of things, including more notice before visiting accounts, establishment of accounting teams versus new teams for each account, monthly office updates, ordering three specific accounting journals, changing the place of the office Christmas party, and allowing staff input into the annual plan. There were also many specific ideas like changing the office set-up, getting a water cooler, and changing how supplies are allocated.

What became clear from this exercise is that most staff are realistic. They know what would improve their work life. They also know the limitations of their employer. When employees are approached in a respectful and honest manner, they tend to be fair and reasonable.

What will you expect to learn from asking them? First, they will list efforts that respond to the very individual needs of each employee—change of hours, learning new skills, ability to change a task. Second, you will find efforts that respond more to the collective needs of employees—regular team meetings, weekly updates, support group, such as that for single parents.

Even though your employees come up with ideas that tend to be realistic and fair, you will not do everything they have identified. But you now have the information that will allow you to work with either individual employees or the group as a whole.

Be open. Be honest and be flexible. They know that everything can't be done. But, if they see you working toward making some of the things happen, they will both respect and appreciate all that you are doing.

> At a large home care organization in a major metropolitan area, I asked, "Name all the things that could be done to improve your quality of work life." Of over 60 items identified by the staff, only four related to salaries. When the management team reviewed all of the requests, it was surprised that more than half could be easily implemented within weeks.

Responding to the Professional Needs of Staff

As the employees' manager, you may be in a much better position to identify and respond to the professional needs of your staff. There are two ways you can approach this; by encouraging staff to identify areas in which they would like to improve professionally and by incorporating professional development into the performance appraisal process of your organization.

Helping staff define their professional development needs. As employees evolve through their careers, they are normally aware of their strengths, of what they do well. It is no surprise that they are proud of these strengths and often focus on them. Most people like to feel good about themselves. By building on their strengths, they can experience success.

At the same time, however, most employees are aware of areas where they lack strength. They may be struggling in task or skills areas. Or there might be areas of success where they could improve their performance through training or support. Whatever the reason, these are areas in which the employee would appreciate the opportunity to have new experiences or to learn new skills.

There is also a third area—skills in which an employee may be weak but is unaware of the weakness or unaware that skills are even needed. Whatever the reason for the employee not knowing, you, as the manager, know it and you have the responsibility to let the employee know.

Your challenge as that employee's manager is to work with the employee to identify those areas of professional development in which the employee is interested or needs to learn or improve upon his or her skills. Zero in on the ones that make the most sense and are most responsive to the employee's desire or need.

What are some examples of professional development activities that might be identified by employees? In many cases, they are job or industry specific. They might include learning some new technology, training in a new procedure or process, or learning new skills. It could also mean having the opportunity to participate in learning planning skills through agency planning efforts or problem solving efforts. It could even mean learning how to interact with other departments or the larger community by representing either the department or the organization.

Not all areas of professional development have to be in job-specific skills. The importance of basic workplace skills that employees will need as the nation moves into the 21st century is probably best exemplified by a major two-year study conducted by the US Department of Labor and the American Society of Training and Development. Researchers found that a number of generic skills were essential for employees to learn in the future. They range from communication skills to problem solving to personal development. As the researchers pointed out, "today's workplace requires employees to have not only the standard academic skills . . . but also other key basics as a foundation for building more sophisticated job-related skills." [5]

Whatever the skill or experience sought by employees, managers should focus on two things: help them refine and clarify what they would like to do and find ways to help them receive the necessary training and support.

Incorporating professional development into the supervisory process. Professional development of an employee is especially helpful as part of regular supervision. It is not a matter that you have to work out with an employee in a single session. It often works far more effectively if it is addressed over a number of sessions. Jointly, you can come up with a list of skills or training that you believe would further the employee's professional development. You then can work within the realities of the organization to provide the opportunities.

Even in a very tight and limiting organization, creative supervisors can find ways to respond to the needs of their employees. You may have only to bring in some articles or loan an employee a book. Or it may mean that you will invite the employee to certain types of meetings. Or it may mean that you will ensure that an employee gets the needed training.

You can be assured that your employees will appreciate your concern. Who among us doesn't appreciate it when our supervisor takes a positive interest in us and works to provide us with opportunities that make our job more professionally rewarding? The supervisory session is one of the best times to do this.

Incorporating professional development into the personal appraisal process. The second but possibly more effective way to approach professional development is more formal. It is also a means to dramatically enhance the performance appraisal process.

WHAT IS THE PERFORMANCE APPRAISAL PROCESS?

Years ago, the performance appraisal process was called the employee evaluation. Today we've increased the sophistication of the process, added better criteria and measurement tools, and made the overall process clearer and more helpful to both employee and organization. But when you get down to it, it is still a system for evaluating employee performance.

A performance appraisal should never be a surprise. You should never save up negative comments to "hit the employee during the evaluation." If you were ever surprised by your supervisor's comments when you were being appraised, then you were the victim of a lousy manager. If you've ever done that to an employee, now is the time to discontinue a flawed management practice.

Joanne worked in a small manufacturing company that supplied specialized parts to the energy field. She was a person who had succeeded—in fact excelled—in every job she had. During her performance review, she was heavily criticized for faulty calculations used in a specific reporting system. She asked her supervisor (who had been aware that she was doing it wrong for six weeks) why she was being told now rather than when she first started doing it. He responded that he planned to discuss it with her, but since her evaluation was coming up, he thought he would do it more formally at that time. Joanne was demoralized by the process and out of frustration left the organization.

Performance appraisals should simply be an accurate summation of feedback that the employee has already received. If employees are doing something wrong, they should hear about it immediately, not at the performance appraisal.

If your feedback system and performance appraisal process are in harmony, the appraisal itself should be mostly positive. Employees should get constructive feedback immediately and in an ongoing manner. With the right supervisory support, they should be correcting their performance. The performance appraisal should be acknowledging and supporting the changes they've made.

Flaws in the Performance Appraisal System

There is an inherent flaw in most performance appraisal systems: they tend to focus on the past and present and very little on the future. In essence, they say here's what you've done over the past year and here's where you are now. Employees interested in progressing farther and in moving up in their organization normally get very little insight from the appraisal into what they need to do to advance professionally.

Howard was in a rage. He had just been rejected for a promotion. He was waving his latest performance appraisal in the face of his supervisor. "It is an exceptional appraisal," said Howard. "You even said it was one of the best you've ever given," he reminded him. "How could I have been rejected when I performed so well?"

The supervisor responded, "Howard, the appraisal is an accurate appraisal of your performance on the job you're in, not on the job the next level up. There are some skills needed in the next level that you never learned." All Howard could say was, "Why didn't you tell me? I would have taken courses and learned the skills."

Most performance appraisals do not tell the employee being appraised what skills they must learn to progress in the organization. It's not only unfair to the employee but can be unfair to the organization. The employee never receives direction on how to grow professionally. The organization loses the opportunity to ensure that present employees are growing and learning the skills needed to lead the organization into the future.

There is an answer. It's called the Professional Development Form (see Chart 3.1). It is part of the performance appraisal process. While the performance appraisal process focuses on past performances and present status, the Professional Development Form addresses the future needs, expectations, and aspirations of employees.

Using a Professional Development Form

The Professional Development Form actually responds to the needs of two types of employees.

1. Employees who want to know what skills or experience they need to advance in the organization.
2. Employees who are interested in having new experiences or learning new skills as part of their own professional development, independent from their desire to advance in the organization.

Chart 3.1 *Employee Professional Development Form*

We are firmly committed to supporting the personal and professional development of each of our employees. As part of our commitment to you, we would like to help you identify areas in which you would like to improve yourself personally and professionally and assist you in achieving your goals in these areas.

This form is designed to assist you in this process. It requires that you clarify your personal and professional needs, identify as concretely as possible how these needs can be best met, and define how your supervisor can best support your efforts. This form should be initially developed by you and jointly refined by you and your supervisor. Upon joint approval, both you and your supervisor should sign the form.

1. Your Name: _____

2. Please list the areas in which you would like to receive training and/or personal and professional support.

   _____

   _____

3. Please list the specific means in which your training and personal and professional needs will be met. Be as specific as possible.

   _____

   _____

4. Please list how your supervisor will support your efforts to receive the training and support that you have identified.

   _____

   _____

5. Quarterly dates in which you and your supervisor will review your progress and ensure that you are receiving the training and support that you desire, and doing so in a manner that meets your joint expectations.

   First Quarter: _____   Third Quarter: _____

   Second Quarter: _____   Fourth Quarter: _____

Approved

_____   _____
Date   Date

_____   _____
Your Name   Supervisor

As an employee's manager, you must work with the employee to answer three key questions when using the Professional Development Form.

1. What training or professional development experiences would the employee like to have? The answer to this question will come from your feedback to the employee on what they need to learn or experience in order to advance in the organization. It will also come from ideas by the employee on what they would like to learn. Together—and this is critical—together you will define the specific skills or experiences the employee should receive.

2. How will the employee learn the skills or have the new experiences? This general question raises a host of specific questions concerning employees. Will they go to specific training programs? Will you or someone else train them? Will they be assigned to a new group? Will you arrange for certain publications or films to be purchased by the organization? Whatever process you use, be explicit.

3. How will you as the manager support and ensure that the effort will happen? This question, which may be the most important question, needs to be answered once you have jointly defined what the employee will be learning and the means in which the new learning will be provided.

This step is the most important for ensuring the success of the professional development effort. You share in the employee's efforts and become committed to doing what is necessary to help the employee. It also sends a message to the employee: I can and I am willing to do whatever it takes to support your professional development.

Examples of Professional Development Efforts

The list of types of professional development efforts is unlimited. It reflects the reality that individual employees have individual needs. The list also tends to parallel lists made by employees who individually identify areas in which they would like to improve their professional development. For example, you and your employee may realize that the employee could benefit from training in new job skills. It could be technical training or how to use a new computer system or computer program.

In other cases, the training might be on functions normally done by people in higher positions. For people interested in moving up to management you may decide that it would be helpful if the employee begins to learn how to support or supervise employees, particularly those new to their positions. You could arrange for them to begin mentoring one or two new staff members or an intern. Or you might want them to gain experience working in groups through co-leading a group supervision session. You might have them join a task force or an organization problem solving group. If you are using total quality management, you could point out a leadership role on an aspect of the program.

There will be some obvious gaps when you and the employee begin working on the professional development plan. Use the plan to provide opportunities to learn skills or have experiences to address their weak areas. If their overall performance is consistently strong, the performance development plan should focus on opportunities to enhance professional development. The plan should not be developed in a single meeting, because it may take two or three meetings to identify ways to improve the professional development of the employee before the plan can be finalized. This time allows both you and the employee to think about options slowly and methodically. Follow-up meetings on the options to be used in the professional development plan can be incorporated into regularly scheduled supervisory sessions.

DIFFERENCES BETWEEN BEHAVIORS

One question frequently raised is how does personal and professional development differ from directive behavior and work-specific support? There are two major differences.

Directive behavior and work-specific support focus on the task itself. Personal and professional development focus more on the needs of the individual. The manager helps the employee successfully learn the skills needed to do the job and supports the employee on the job itself. While the process of learning enhances the professional development of the employee, the focus is clearly on ensuring that the employee has the competence and motivation to do the job in a qualitative and professional manner.

In personal and professional development, the focus is on the manager's effective response to the personal and professional needs of the employee.

Directive behavior and work-specific support are manager driven. Personal and professional development are either employee driven or jointly driven by the employee and manager. When providing directive behavior and work-specific support, the manager usually assesses the situation and takes a leadership role in either defining what the employee should be doing or supporting the employee's efforts.

In personal and professional development support, the focus is on helping define the employee's professional needs and then working with the employee to meet those needs. Again, the manager and employee work together to define the best ways to help the employee improve professionally. Unlike when providing directive behavior and work-specific support, where the focus is on the specific job, the focus of the manager is on working with the employee to find better ways to support the employee and to enhance his or her professional development.

Does this mean that personal and professional development is not concerned with the employee's job or tasks? Of course not. Most of the focus will be clearly associated with work, but by responding to the employee's personal and professional needs the manager makes a more competent and contented employee, one who is more committed and supportive to the overall efforts and goals of the organization.

Responding to Higher Functioning Employees

If an employee is struggling or has not learned the basic skills to do the job, it makes little sense for a manager to focus support on responding to his or her personal needs or providing the employee with professional development opportunities. Personal and professional development support is far more appropriate for higher functioning employees. This is one of the key premises of the Functional Management Model.

Personal and professional development support begins to make sense as employees prove their competence on the job itself. It is clearly more appropriate to reward these employees by responding to their personal needs, professional development, and potential for advancement. Obviously, support for higher functioning employees reinforces the organization's commitment to the employee and increases the likelihood that these employees stay committed to the organization.

The Foundation for the Functional Management Model

Together the three major supervisory management skills—directive behavior, work-specific support, and personal and professional development support—provide managers with the foundation for being exceptional supervisors. However, knowing the skills is not enough. You need to know when to use them. Are there times that you should use all three? Are there times when one of these skills is more appropriate than another? What relation do these behaviors have to the functional level of a specific employee? Are there any clarifying rules for a manager to follow in achieving maximum levels of performance and commitment by employees who function at different levels?

The answers are found in the full Functional Management Model. What you have learned are the basic behaviors needed to be an effective supervisory manager. Before you can apply one, all, or a combination of these behaviors, however, you must have a means of differentiating among employees; that is, you must first determine how each of your employees is functioning. Chapter 4 provides a simple but highly effective means for accurately assessing the functional level of your employees.

HOW GOOD ARE YOU?

The challenge to becoming an exceptional supervisory manager is not in learning the six goals of supervision or in learning the three major skills that are essential to that. The real challenge is in determining how effective you are utilizing each of the three key supervisory skills. Do you have good directive behavior? Do you provide clear directions? Does your staff understand clearly what you want done?

Chart 3.2 *Management Plus Supervisory Effectiveness Survey*

Please rate how well your supervisor does on the following dimensions. The higher the score, the more effective the supervisor.

My supervisor

1. Provides clear direction whenever asking me to do something.

| Low 1 | 2 | 3 | 4 | 5 | 6 | 7 High |

2. Asks me to repeat what I am expected to do to ensure that I understand instructions clearly.

| Low 1 | 2 | 3 | 4 | 5 | 6 | 7 High |

3. Provides me with training for skills that I need to do the job successfully.

| Low 1 | 2 | 3 | 4 | 5 | 6 | 7 High |

4. Helps me to understand how my efforts fit into the big picture.

| Low 1 | 2 | 3 | 4 | 5 | 6 | 7 High |

5. Holds regularly scheduled supervisory sessions with me.

| Low 1 | 2 | 3 | 4 | 5 | 6 | 7 High |

6. Provides me with immediate feedback on my performance.

| Low 1 | 2 | 3 | 4 | 5 | 6 | 7 High |

7. Ensures that I receive ongoing encouragement and support in the work that I do.

| Low 1 | 2 | 3 | 4 | 5 | 6 | 7 High |

8. Personally models the type of work and performance that is expected of me.

| Low 1 | 2 | 3 | 4 | 5 | 6 | 7 High |

9. Seeks ways to help me address appropriate work-related personal needs.

| Low 1 | 2 | 3 | 4 | 5 | 6 | 7 High |

10. Works with me to identify ways that the organization can help me enhance my professional development.

| Low 1 | 2 | 3 | 4 | 5 | 6 | 7 High |

Average score: _____

What about work-specific support? Do you provide regularly scheduled supervision for each of your employees? Do you give them feedback in a timely manner? Do you provide them with ongoing support and encouragement?

And the third major supervisory skill—personal and professional development support. Do you seek ways to help your higher functioning employees in matters of personal needs and professional development?

The Management Plus Supervisory Effectiveness Survey (Chart 3.2) identifies a number of supervisory behaviors related to the three key skills and provides you with the means to rate how well you actually do in each behavior. The 10 items in the questionnaire do not represent everything that can or should be measured. They do, however, represent major behaviors that are generally found in exceptional supervisors. Additional qualities could be added to the list. Note that questions 9 and 10 are more appropriate for higher functioning employees. You may wish to exclude them when questioning all your employees. You can use this questionnaire in two ways—one easy and one tough.

1. *The easy or safe way.* Rate yourself. Look at each of the behaviors and rate how well you do them. This is subjective in nature, but it gives you the chance to reflect on your own performance and identify your strengths or weaknesses.

2. *The tough but more objective way.* Ask your staff to rate you. They really know how effective you are as a supervisor. If you think that you give clear direction and they think you don't, then from a staff perspective your directions are not clear. Because your goal is to provide clear directions that your staff understand, their feedback will let you know just how good you really are.

Both ways your average score should be 5.5 or better. A score between 3.5 and 5.5 is transitional—you could get better or you could get worse. A score of 3 or less means trouble. You need to improve your performance.

Chapter Four

How to Assess the Functional Levels of Your Employees

T here is a misconception about supervision that sounds great. It is so generally accepted that most managers consider it a "supervisory truism." It goes something like this:

> The best supervisors are those who are consistent; they treat all employees the same. They don't play favorites. It doesn't matter if the employee is a personal friend or someone whom they see only at work; everyone will be treated the same. New employees are not abused. It doesn't matter if an employee has been around for 10 weeks or 10 years. Everyone can expect the same treatment, the same support, the same direction, and the same levels of encouragement. There are no favorites.

Sounds good, doesn't it, almost like motherhood and apple pie? A manager who plays no favorites. The trouble is, it's wrong. More accurately, the implementation of this supposed truism is wrong, sometimes disastrously wrong.

THE FALLACY OF FAIRNESS

To become an exceptional manager, it is important that you understand what is wrong with the supposed truism. It contains one serious flaw: it focuses on the manager and is almost devoid of any consideration of the employee.

Think about the staff you supervise. Are they all the same? Are they different in any way? Do all of them have the same skills and the same expertise? Are they equally motivated? Your answer: "No, all of my staff are not the same."

Now consider if all of your staff are not the same, does it make sense for you to treat them all in the same manner? Wouldn't you treat staff who function at lower levels in a different way than staff who are high achievers and performers? Wouldn't it make sense that staff who lack skills would be treated in a different way than employees who are highly skilled? And wouldn't you respond differently to your motivated staff than to employees who lack motivation?

A DIFFERENCE IN MEANING

Because employees are not the same, it makes no sense to treat them all the same. This doesn't mean that you treat some employees more fairly than others. The terms *fairly* and *the same* do not have the same meaning. Fairly means that you treat all staff respectfully. Treating staff the same means that all staff will be treated identically. What you do for your most knowledgeable employees and highest performers would be what you would do for your least knowledgeable employees and lowest achievers. Obviously this doesn't make sense.

As a manager, training is the fairest thing that you can do with an employee struggling to learn the skills required of the job. That treatment is fair to struggling employees, but inappropriate for your high performers who had mastered the skills long ago.

The real trouble with the truism is that it views supervisory management from a static or structured perspective. Unfortunately, it is devoid of the reality that the best supervision is that which is sensitive to the individual needs and levels of functioning of each employee, and which provides support responsive to the level of functioning of individual employees.

The best managers know how well their staff are performing and functioning. They have made assessments based on an objective analysis of the individual employee's performance. How they supervise and support each employee depends on how they assess the employee's functional level. The response of the manager will vary according to employee performance levels. The real challenge you face as a manager is determining the functional levels of your employees.

MEASURING HOW WELL YOUR EMPLOYEES ARE FUNCTIONING

How can you be an effective supervisor unless you have some way of objectively determining how your employees are functioning on the job or know what their needs are?

It is important to have some type of conceptual understanding to objectively assess your employees and their level of functioning. A conceptual understanding provides you with a wonderful means for quickly and accurately categorizing the level of functioning of individual employees. It gives you the foundation for developing consistent strategies for responding effectively to employees at roughly the same levels of functioning.

Once you know how to measure how well each of your employees is functioning, you can provide them with the right types of support. You can use your time and resources wisely and effectively. A solid conceptual understanding enables you to know which employees need more training and technical support and which need more motivational support. You also will have the means and rationale for differentiating your higher functioning employees from those who have not reached that level. And as soon as you know how to measure each of your employees and have determined why they are assessed at a particular level, you can supervise them in a manner that brings them to their optimal levels of functioning and performance.

Problems with Developing an Optimal Assessment Tool

A truly helpful assessment tool must not be limited to certain types of employees or certain types of jobs. It must be applicable both to women and men, college graduates and school dropouts, and high wage earners and low earners. It must be applicable to all races, all ages, all backgrounds, and all types of industries.

The assessment tool must also be practical, easy to learn, and easy to use. Assessment strategies that require you to complete a 500-page employee questionnaire or that require the employee to take a battery of psychological tests make no sense. For most supervisors, such assessment tools, while valid, are too cumbersome.

A truly helpful assessment tool has to be user-friendly, a tool that any manager can learn and apply easily. It can't be filled with exceptions or complex interpretations. It should work with both longtime and new employees. It should be as effective in measuring the functional levels of high performers as it is with marginal performers. Finally, it should be a tool that allows you to differentiate between employees based on easily observable and measurable concrete standards.

Learning from Former Management Models

The best supervisory management models recognize and build on the strengths of former models. In developing the Functional Management Model, I learned that management theorists and practitioners took major strides in advancing the practice of supervisory management every generation or two. Since the early 1900s, management theorists have changed the focus of supervisory management from supervisors to employees. Frederick W. Taylor, recognized as the father of modern management, coined the term *scientific management*.[1] Taylor articulated a form of management in which the manager structured the work and provided employees with systematic instructions on how to do each task in order to achieve maximum levels of efficiency and productivity.

Some twenty years following Taylor's work, researchers from Harvard University raised managers to a new level. In their experiments at the Western Electric plant in Hawthorne, Illinois, researchers led by Elton Mayo discovered that when managers paid additional attention to their employees, productivity went up.[2]

While Taylor stressed the need to organize employees to gain higher levels of productivity, Mayo's group found that productivity and motivation could also be increased through recognition and personal support of employees.

In the late 1940s and 1950s, Douglas McGregor carried this thinking one step further with his Theory X–Theory Y view of management (see Chapter 2). Basically, as a quick review, McGregor postulated that managers' attitudes about employees fell between two extremes, Theory X and Theory Y, of how supervisors theoretically viewed employees. Theory X managers were marked as managers with a somewhat rigid view toward employees—as inherently lazy, consistently avoiding work, with lit-tle desire for responsibility, and little capacity for creativity. These managers needed to closely monitor and control staff. Theory Y managers viewed employees much differently. They saw employ-ees as more creative, self-motivated, and willing to accept respon-sibility under proper conditions.

McGregor felt that how a manager relates to and supervises employees is often the result of how they view employees. Super-visors who viewed their employees from a positive, or Theory Y, point of view tended to be more committed to empowering their employees and involving them in decision making and problem solving. Those supervisors who were more skeptical tended to be more controlling and more autocratic in their behavior.

McGregor focused on the supervisor rather than the employee. The supervisor's positive or negative attitude toward employees shaped the treatment they got. Employee motivation responded to this supervisory behavior and, of course, the attitude behind it. Supervisors who viewed their employees in a more positive light naturally tended to get higher levels of commitment and motiva-tion.[3]

What McGregor didn't do was to provide a means for managers to have a more objective view of the functional level of employees. That advancement was left to two professors from Ohio State University, Ken Blanchard and Paul Hersey, who conducted ex-tensive research in the field of leadership. They postulated that two leadership behaviors—task behaviors and maintenance be-haviors—could be used in supervising and motivating employees. They also presented a model for assessing the functional level of employees.[4]

Hersey and Blanchard discovered that how well an employee functions on the job depends on two variables: the employee's ability and motivation. They suggested that employees in the same job might differ in their ability and motivational levels, a logical premise that served as one of the foundations of their internationally recognized Situational Leadership Model®. Blan-chard and Hersey advanced supervisory management forward by providing a simple yet effective way to assess the functional levels of employees, an approach that the Functional Management Model clearly recognizes.

ASSESSING THE EMPLOYEE'S FUNCTIONAL LEVEL

Ability and motivation are easy to assess and they are observable. As variables they make sense to managers. Think about it. If you want an employee to do a job, what does he or she need to have? Answer: the ability to do it. If the employee lacks or is weak in one of the two variables, the job won't get done.

If the employee doesn't have the skills, he obviously can't do the job. If the employee has the skills but isn't motivated or willing to do it, the job is not going to get done. If the employee has neither the skills nor the motivation, can you guess what's going to happen? Not much.

Again, the point is that the two variables, ability and motivation, provide an excellent way to assess the functional levels of each member of your staff. They also provide a key component of the Functional Management Model.

Defining the Two Employee Functioning Variables

Before you can use the two variables, you need working definitions.

Ability:

Having the skills and knowledge needed to do the job in a qualitative and timely fashion.

Motivation:

Being self-driven, willing, and committed to doing the job in a qualitative and timely fashion.

Both definitions include the phrase, "qualitative and timely fashion," because in today's highly competitive environment it is no longer acceptable to do poor quality work or to complete a task after the deadline. Within the total quality management movement, providing high-quality products and services in a timely manner is not only the best thing, it is the only acceptable thing to do.

Defining the Four Employee Functional Levels

Assuming that employees have either high or low ability and either high or low motivation, it is clear that employees function at any one of four possible levels:

F-1: Low Ability/Low Motivation

F-2: Low Ability/High Motivation

F-3: High Ability/Low Motivation

F-4: High Ability/High Motivation

Realistically, an employee will not be simply high or low on either ability or motivation. He or she could be medium, medium-high, medium-low, or at some other point on the spectrum. What managers prefer, however, is that employees be high on both variables and they strive to help them achieve that goal. Managers recognize that when an employee is not high in both dimensions, they must adopt a strategy that provides the necessary support and supervision. The low and high categories simply make it easier for us to differentiate one type of employee from another. They provide you with a highly practical, user-friendly model for assessing the functional level of employees and for determining appropriate supervisory approaches.

It is important to understand each of the four functional levels and to explore how employees tend to evolve within a specific job.

F-1 employees: low ability/low motivation. For many managers, the F-1 employee is the worst kind of employee—one who lacks the skills to do the job in a qualitative and timely fashion. To make matters worse, F-1 employees are usually not very willing or motivated to do the work or learn the skills.

John was frustrated, angry, disillusioned, and demoralized. He had worked for the State Revenue Department for nearly 14 years. He loved what he did and was really good at it. Everything was fine until the state's economy bottomed out, resulting in massive state layoffs and reassignments.

John was one of the lucky ones. He didn't lose his job, but because of his 14 years of seniority he was given the added responsibility to make up for the work done by those who were laid off. To make matters worse, the state implemented a new computerized reconciliation system. John had never worked with computers before and was really struggling.

In less than six months, John found himself moving from being a highly competent professional to one who felt overworked and overwhelmed learning his job all over again. He lost enthusiasm and motivation. His ideal job had become drudgery.

How someone becomes an F-1 employee differs from employee to employee. Some are hired for jobs that they can't seem to learn; slowly they become demoralized and unmotivated. Others might have been forced into a job that they didn't want. Still others might be like John—excellent employees thrust suddenly into a position that overwhelms them and requires skills that they find difficult to learn.

Whatever the reason, one thing is certain. F-1 employees lack both the ability and motivation to do the job. An organization dominated by F-1 employees will not be around very long.

F-2 employees: low ability/high motivation. I often think of F-2 employees as a supervisor's dream. They want to be there. They are motivated. They want to learn. They are committed to succeeding.

True, they presently lack the ability to do the job. They will need to learn the skills required to do the job in a qualitative and timely fashion. In some cases, they might need to learn a great number of skills to succeed on the job. But because F-2 employees are very special, a manager who knows how to support them with appropriate support and training will see them become a real asset to the organization.

Diana was thrilled. She had recently applied for and got a job as a graphic designer at a major advertising firm in New York. It was perfect, the type of job she always wanted to do in the city she always wanted to live in. Even the salary—although not tremendous—was certainly acceptable.

The first four weeks on the job told her two things. First, she was going to need to learn a great deal in order to succeed on the job. Expectations were high and so were standards and demands. Second, and equally clear, was that the organization was committed to supporting and training its employees. Her

supervisor gave her support and encouragement. She also took
the time to identify the skills that Diana needed to learn, and
arranged and scheduled the training to learn the skills. It was
no wonder that Diana remained excited and motivated to do
the job.

For Diana, the excitement and motivation came because it was a
new job. If you think about it, almost all new employees are F-2
employees. They've got a job to which they were promoted or
applied and are generally pleased and motivated to make a success
of themselves. What more could a supervisor ask for?

New employees are not the only F-2 employees. Reenergized
and remotivated F-1 employees may develop into F-2 employees.
So may employees who are in the same job but have been given
new roles and responsibilities.

F-3 employees: high ability/low motivation. The employees to worry about most are F-3 employees. These are usually
employees who have worked for you for some time. They know
the skills needed to succeed on the job, and they clearly have the
ability to do it. The problem is that they lack the enthusiasm and
motivation to do the job in a qualitative and timely manner.

F-3 employees are particularly difficult to deal with because,
although they have the ability and have learned the skills, they do
just enough to get by. Their lack of enthusiasm and low-energy
performances often have a negative impact on the team.

Twenty-four years! That's how long Frank had worked at the
bank. When he first joined the bank, his rise up the career ladder
had been steady and predictable. Trainee to assistant treasurer to
treasurer to assistant branch manager. Seven years ago he was
named branch manager. Then things came to a halt. A
slowdown in the banking industry and two mergers made it
clear to Frank that he'd be branch manager for some time, maybe
forever.

There has been one word going through Frank's mind for the
past two years: BORING! The job was becoming very boring, the
same things day in, day out. With no challenges on the horizon,
it was difficult for Frank to be excited or motivated to do the job.

In many ways, Frank found himself doing just enough to get
by. In a few cases, he let things go or didn't get reports in on

time. He seemed to have lost enthusiasm and motivation and rarely looked forward to coming to work.

The term used to describe this type of employee is *burnout*. Frank is burned out. He lacks motivation. He lacks enthusiasm. He seems to be sliding by.

Burnout is a terrible term that has been a disservice to many fine employees. I'll challenge that term later, but for the present I acknowledge that burnout has been used to label F-3 employees.

F-3 employees are not the only employees to be labeled burned out. Others include F-1 employees who might have learned many of the skills to succeed on the job slowly. They may continue to lack the motivation or enthusiasm to do the job, but by virtue of learning the skills they can evolve to an F-3 level of functioning.

F-3 employees are not always long-term employees or those who have evolved from an F-1 level. Some may be F-3 employees new to an organization who discover that they have taken a job that is not very challenging. They might have thought they were moving into a higher, more challenging position, or they might have felt that they were misled. Whatever the reason, F-3 employees often feel underutilized and underchallenged, and they slowly lose their motivation and enthusiasm.

F-4 employees: high ability/high motivation.   If any employee is a manager's dream, it's got to be the F-4 employee. They usually love their jobs. They know their jobs and have the skills and knowledge to succeed.

F-4 employees are also highly motivated. They want to do the job. They are self-driven. They enjoy what they do and are highly committed to doing it right.

Managers can really rely on F-4 employees. They always come through because they know what to do and they like doing it. Managers hope all staff could achieve this level of functioning.

As Elaine reflected on her past five years as special education director of a medium-size school system, one thought struck her: I surely am fortunate to have a job that I love.

True, Elaine had worked hard to learn the skills needed to succeed on the job. She had always worked and had chosen to go to night school to finish her master's degree in special education administration. It was hard, sometimes grueling, but she hung in and eventually obtained her degree. She also took advantage of the support she received from her supervisor and never avoided training opportunities made available to her.

Elaine was a success on her job. She was recognized as being a highly skilled, highly motivated professional. She may have felt lucky to have her present job, but there was no question she'd earned it.

Elaine represents the type of employee you all want to have. She is also the type of employee you all want to be—highly skilled and highly motivated.

Employees like Elaine don't just happen. They are the product of hard work and dedication by both themselves and their past and present direction supervisors. If Elaine had not been provided with the appropriate levels of direction, work-specific support, and personal and professional development support, she may never have grown into the employee she is today.

The questions managers hoping to develop and maintain employees like Elaine should ask are: "How can I best supervise and support my employees so that they become exceptional F-4 employees? What levels of direction and work-specific support should I provide? What forms of personal and professional development would be most responsive to this employee's needs?

These questions are at the heart of the Functional Management Model. When you know the functional level of your employees, the Functional Management Model will provide you with logical, highly practical answers to how to best supervise, motivate, and support each of them.

HOW FUNCTIONAL LEVELS EVOLVE
AND CHANGE

Because employees are not static and tend to function differently over the time they serve in a specific job, the obvious question that managers must ask is, "How do employees evolve on the job?"

But do employees tend to stay in the same functional level in a specific job throughout their career? I suppose if you have characterized some of your employees as F-1, F-2, or F-3, you are probably saying, "I hope not." But you are certainly hoping that your F-4 employees will. The good or bad news, depending on how you look at it, is that all employees have the real potential to change their level of functioning. Therefore your goal as a supervisor is to help your F-1, F-2, and F-3 employees either learn the skills or become more motivated in order to evolve to the F-4 level. For F-4 employees, your goal obviously is to find ways for them to maintain their exemplary performance. In the forthcoming chapters, you'll find concrete answers for dealing effectively with the four types of employees.

A Logical Evolution

If you think about it, employees do not evolve from an F-1 level to F-2 to F-3 to F-4. It's not logical. An employee who functions at an F-1 level (low ability/low motivation) may become reenergized and remotivated and evolve to an F-2 level (low ability/high motivation). And if the employee stays motivated and eventually learns the appropriate skills, he or she will evolve from an F-2 level to F-4 (high ability/high motivation). The employee would not evolve to an F-3 level (high ability/low motivation). It doesn't make sense. Do you think an F-2 employee who finally learns the skills to succeed on the job will then become demotivated? Not likely.

In analyzing the logical evolution of employees, a graphic model helps show the relationship among the four employee func-

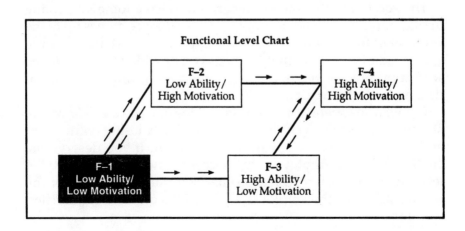

tional levels. Employee functioning is not an unrealistic evolution from F-1 to F-4, but has more of a multidimensional reality.

Let's look again at the four types of employees to better appreciate how they evolve on the job from their present level to an F-4 level.

F-1 employees: low ability/low motivation. They either make it or they don't. There are two ways that they can evolve to the F-4 level. The first and more common way is to move up to the F-2 level by becoming more energized and more motivated. Assuming they have the ability to learn, these employees can eventually learn the job and evolve from F-2 to F-4.

The second way occurs when F-1 employees slowly begin to learn the skills needed to succeed and evolve to the F-3 level. As they experience more and more success on the task itself, they gain enthusiasm and motivation and slowly evolve to the F-4 level.

F-2 employees: low ability/high motivation. This is a good news/bad news scenario. The good news is that F-2 employees who learn the skills they need to succeed can evolve from the F-2 to the F-4 level.

The bad news scenario is just the opposite. Although the F-2 employees start out being highly motivated, they don't learn or are unable to learn the skills needed to succeed. As they continue to experience failure, they become demoralized, lose their motivation, and evolve to the F-1 level.

The good news/bad news scenarios also have some interesting implications for you. For example, if the employee moves up to the F-4 level of functioning, you, as the supervisor, certainly deserve some credit for making that happen; you provided that employee with appropriate levels of training, supervision, and support. You deserve both the credit and congratulations.

But what happens if the employee doesn't make it. He or she struggles, becomes overwhelmed, and, slowly losing enthusiasm and motivation, slides down to the F-1 level. If you deserve the credit for the F-2 employee who succeeds and evolves to the F-4 level, doesn't it stand to reason that you must take some of the responsibility for the employee's failing? No one said supervision was easy.

F-3 employees: high ability/low motivation. There is only one direction for these employees to go. Since they already have the skills to do the job, the issue is motivation.

Employees might become rusty in skills that they have not used, but they won't lose them. If they are going to evolve to the F-4 level, they will need either to regain their motivation to succeed (if they lost it) or, for the employee who has evolved to the F-3 level from the F-1 level, gain it for the first time. Once they do, they will evolve to the F-4 level.

F-4 employees: high ability/high motivation. These are the employees that you don't want to lose. F-4 employees are already highly skilled and motivated. As their supervisor, the only thing that you want is for these employees to maintain their motivation and continue as model employees. Your ultimate challenge (see Chapter 8) is to determine how to best maintain the enthusiasm and motivation of F-4 employees.

Knowing how employees evolve is critical to effective supervision and it is one of the major components of the Functional Management Model. There are, however, a number of important points related to working with employee functional levels.

Three Rules to Functional Levels

One of the great things about the functional levels is that they give you an easy way to assess the performance status of any of your employees. They also give you some sense of how your employees will most likely evolve. However, you need to keep these points in mind.

1. Employees have a predominate level. Your employees are not 100 percent of any level. F-4 employees are not highly skilled and highly motivated in every aspect of their job. An employee may be a superstar in every aspect of his or her job but hate paperwork. For most of the job, the employee functions at the F-4 level, in paperwork, at an F-3 or even an F-1 level. The key point is that despite having traces of all four levels, employees tend to function primarily at one.

2. An employee's functional level has a relationship to a specific job. If an employee is functioning at the F-4 level and is promoted or changes jobs, you must reassess both the employee's motivation and skill level in relation to the new job. Normally when an employee, including an F-4 employee, moves to a new job, new skills must be learned. On the new job, the employee is therefore functioning at an F-2 level until the skills are learned and the employee evolves back to an F-4 level. Employee levels must be determined according to the present job, not in terms of previous jobs.

3. Employees are not static but tend to evolve on the job. Employees are not stuck in a specific functional level; they have the potential of evolving in both positive and negative directions. From a supervisory perspective, however, it is important to realize that employees do change. Supervisors must help lower functioning employees mature to the F-4 level and help F-4 level employees maintain their high levels of performance.

The Functional Level Chart and the functional model of assessment are exciting and highly practical ways to better understand the employees you supervise. The key to effective supervision is knowing your employees. This model provides an excellent means to do this in a simple yet highly effective manner.

What Do the Arrows on the Chart Mean?

Look again at the chart. Notice that the arrows go both ways between F-1 and F-2 and they go both ways between F-3 and F-4. But the arrows go only one way between F-2 and F-4 and between F-1 and F-3. Why?

The answer is simple. It has to do with ability levels. Once employees learn the skills required by the job, they are skilled to do that job. The automobile mechanic who learns how to fix a certain car, knows how to fix the car. Once you learn how to swim, you know how to swim.

The arrows on the Functional Level Chart reflect the fact that employees will not lose skills that they have already learned and will not evolve to a low ability level from high ability levels.

Keep in mind that an employee's functional level is in direct relation to a specific job. Also keep in mind employees might have to periodically brush up on specific aspects of their jobs. Just as someone who learned to ride a bike but hasn't ridden one in a while may have to get used to balancing a bike again, some workers might have to refresh themselves. But neither the bike rider nor the employee has to start from scratch.

The Functional Management Model

Knowing the functional level of employees and knowing how employees evolve is essential to effective supervision. But the real challenge for managers is knowing how to best supervise employees so that they evolve to or maintain the F-4 level of functioning.

When does it make sense to provide extensive direction? How can you best use work-specific support? Which employees would benefit most from personal and professional development support? What combination of supervisory behaviors makes most sense for employees at specific functional levels? How can you get maximum levels of motivation, performance, and commitment from all your employees—particularly when you have different employees functioning at different levels?

These are the questions that are essential to optimal supervision. These questions can best be answered through the Functional Management Model. Now that you've learned the basic supervisory behaviors, know how to assess the functional level of your employees, and understand the four functional levels, you're ready to take the final step . . . to learn the full Functional Management Model.

Chapter Five

Developing the Functional Management Model

It's so frustrating! You've been working with Ruth for nearly two years. She is an employee you like and deeply respect. She was a quick learner and soon became one of your highest and most consistent performers. In fact, for over a year, she was your star employee, one that other employees looked up to and admired. And now this . . .

For the past six months, Ruth has been sliding. Yes, her work seems to be getting done but certainly without the enthusiasm and commitment she used to have. She seems to be marking time without really caring. This has certainly affected your relationship with her and it has had a negative effect on team morale. What should you do? How can you best approach this employee?

Now what? Bill is your worst nightmare. He came to the job with good credentials and the right background. For two years he had worked for another company in a similar job. That company gave him good (although now that you think about it, not great) references. His interview had gone well. He seemed personable and appeared to have the technical understanding of the job. But now . . . .

Bill has been making periodic mistakes and does not alway get his paperwork in on time. When you talked with him about it, he said that the problem lies in the differences between how your company and his former company do things. What really bothers you is that he seems to be taking it all lightly. He doesn't appear to be concerned with the problems or enthused about the job.

And now, his six-month probation period is rapidly coming to an end. You don't want to lose a potentially good worker, but neither do you want to make a permanent employee of someone who may be marginal at best. What do you do? What's the best way for you to approach Bill?

Think of this! An employee who loves to come to work. She is bright, articulate, maybe a little reserved, but clearly an outstanding employee. She loves her work. The quality is always excellent. She's a great team player who is always willing to help her colleagues. When it comes to taking on new challenges and volunteering for something new, she's the first to volunteer.

That's Nina. You couldn't ask for a better employee. Nina's been with you for nearly five years and has slowly emerged as your top performer. Not only is she someone who consistently does a great job, but also she has become a role model for other employees on your team. In fact, she is one of the main reasons that working on your team is so great.

As Nina's supervisor, you worry especially how to keep the job interesting and motivating. In fairness to Nina, you want to supervise her in a way that reinforces your company's commitment to her and that keeps her continually enthused and motivated. How can you best do this? Do you need to make any changes in how you supervise her? What should you consider doing in the future?

DEALING WITH DIFFERENCES

Ruth, Bill, Nina. Three employees working in different organizations. Three employees with different life experiences, talents, and motivation. Three employees who offer their supervisors different kinds of challenges.

Are the situations of Ruth, Bill, and Nina unique? In that they are all individuals with unique feelings, experiences, training, and backgrounds, you have to say yes. But from the perspective of supervisory challenges, you have to say no.

Ruth, Bill, and Nina represent just a few of the challenges presented by millions of employees in the working world. While each relationship between supervisor and employee is unique, these employees present typical problems that managers face on the job every day.

In essence, Ruth, Bill, and Nina are employees who are functioning at different levels. They obviously need different levels of supervisory support and direction. They also provide us with clear examples of what is needed in an ideal supervisory model.

A SHORT REVIEW

Before you put the model together, briefly review the components you need to consider—the functional level of the employee and the combination of supervisory behaviors that the manager can use in supervising the employee.

Functional Levels = Ability + Motivation

Two major factors affect how well an employee functions on a specific job: the amount of ability the employee has to do the job and the employee's level of enthusiasm and motivation on the job itself.

It is important to remember that ability and motivation relate to the employee's specific and present job, not to previous jobs or other parts of his or her life. Nor do they refer to potential. Ability and motivation refer to how an employee is functioning now.

You read in Chapter 4 that employees might have high or low ability and that they also could exhibit high or low motivation. When taken together, four possible employee functional levels emerge:

F-1: Low Ability/Low Motivation

F-2: Low Ability/High Motivation

F-3: High Ability/Low Motivation

F-4: High Ability/High Motivation

To review the four Functional Levels and the directions that employees tend to move while working in a specific job see the functional level chart.

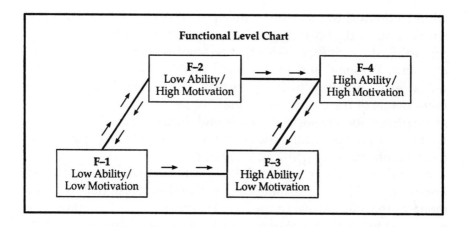

As shown, an employee can move in several directions. An F-1 employee can become motivated and move up to F-2, then learn the needed skills to succeed on the job and move to F-3. Ultimately, the employee can attain the F-4 level.

Employees with high ability normally move between F-3 and F-4 due to one important fact: employees can lose interest and motivation to do the job, but once they learn the skills, they have them. If they don't use the skills, they may get rusty—and they may even need to refresh themselves. But assuming the particular skill doesn't change—or the requirements of the job—it is unnecessary to learn the skills all over again.

These general categories provide you with a simple yet effective means for differentiating employees. They also provide you with the first step of a management rationale: If employees function at different levels, then the supervisor should supervise and support them in different ways.

Three Supervisory Behaviors

A manager can use three major supervisory behaviors to supervise and motivate staff: direction, work-specific support, and personal and professional development support. Each behavior responds to a different need of a specific employee.

Direction provides employees with the training and the expectations required to do the job successfully by telling the employee what to do and training the employee. Work-specific support is supporting and encouraging the employee on the job itself by providing the employee with timely feedback, praise, or encouragement. Personal and professional development support is directed at responding to the personal and professional development needs of the employee by making the job more positive and more professionally supportive through initiating quality of work-life programs or providing the employees with training opportunities to professionally grow and develop.

Note that as the need for work-specific support decreases, the importance of providing more personal and professional development support increases. In the initial stages of a job, the employee may need to learn a number of new skills or procedures and needs a lot of work-specific support. As the employee progresses and learns the skills, less work-specific support and more personal and professional development support are appropriate.

What makes the three supervisory behaviors even more valuable to managers is that they respond to the supervisory goals in optimal supervision. Together, these three behaviors very effectively respond to the supervisory needs of employees.

As you can see in the following table, the three supervisory behaviors are directed at responding to specific needs of employees. By knowing the Functional Levels of employees, you know what their supervisory needs are, and know what supervisory behaviors are most appropriate.

Responding to the Supervisory Needs of Employees

Employee needs	Supervisory response
Training Skill development Task knowledge	Direction
Confidence Encouragement Task motivation	Work-specific support
Challenges Opportunity to learn Personal needs addressed	Personal and professional development support

BEHAVIORAL RESPONSES TO FUNCTIONAL LEVELS

Let's look at each of the four functional levels and identify the logical combination of supervisory behaviors needed to respond to each. You must first identify the functional level of each employee before you can determine the best supervisory behavior. What will emerge is not only a logical and highly practical model for optimal supervision, but also a clear, graphic model that accurately depicts a comprehensive approach to supervision.

The F-1 Employee

Betty Ann used to love to come to work. She had worked at the county credit union for seven years. She enjoyed what she did and with whom she worked. Everything was great until the credit union converted from a manual to a computerized system. Then things began falling apart.

No matter how hard she tried, Betty Ann couldn't master the new system. She couldn't remember the commands. She often merged the wrong files. She constantly made input errors and once accidentally erased a full day's work. She soon dreaded coming to work and was reluctant to turn anything in without checking it over again and again.

At what functional level is Betty Ann? Without question, she is an F-1. She lacks the knowledge and skills to succeed on the new system, making her ability level low. At the same time, because she has had so much difficulty learning the new system with which she has had a number of problems, her confidence and motivational level are also down. So what do you do?

Here the logic behind the Functional Management Model begins to emerge. First, you know that she is having trouble learning the new system. She clearly needs additional training and skill development. High directive behavior is required.

Second, with a low confidence level, Betty Ann obviously needs lots of encouragement and support on the job itself. Her supervisor must give her extensive work-specific support.

What about personal and professional development support? Should the supervisor put a lot of emphasis on this? Of course not. Betty Ann—like all F-1 employees—is struggling to learn and succeed on the job. She needs direction, extensive work-specific support, and little emphasis on personal and professional development support. Ths is an S-1 supervisory approach. Graphically it looks as follows:

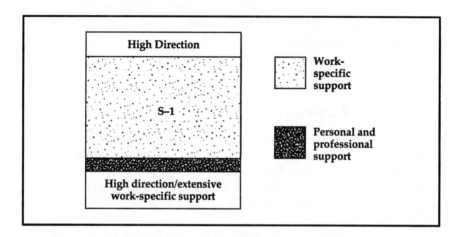

As you can see, the S-1 approach calls for high direction and extensive work-specific support. Rather than excluding personal and professional development support, the graph allows a minimal amount of this type of support because there is always some of this support affecting all staff—for example, organizationwide quality of work life efforts. Also, one component of personal and professional development support is learning new skills. For an F-1 employee, new knowledge and skill development is being provided through high direction.

In Chapter 5, we will focus exclusively on the F-1 employee, reviewing how employees become F-1 employees, and how you can use supervisory strategies to motivate and increase the performance levels of these employees.

The F-2 Employee

What do we know about employees who are at an F-2 functional level? An F-2 employee is someone low on ability and high on motivation. While F-2 employees may lack knowledge or skills in a particular job, they are motivated to learn. Consider the following case study:

Mark had recently been named assistant manager of a large midwestern hotel. He was thrilled. His personal goal since graduating from college was to become a manager of a large hotel and conference center. This job was the perfect stepping-stone.

Mark realized that there was a great deal he had to learn. From scheduling to occupancy quotes to creating a culture of service excellence to conference planing and marketing, there was much he would have to learn. He was looking forward to learning all he could.

Isn't Mark the kind of employee we would all like to recruit—someone highly motivated and anxious to learn? Mark is obviously an F-2 employee—low on ability but high on motivation. What's the best way a manager can supervise an F-2 employee? What supervisory behaviors should a manager use?

If Mark's ability level is low, the most obvious supervisory behavior is high directive behavior. Mark's supervisor must provide him with the training and skill development needed to succeed. At the same time, the supervisor must provide Mark with high work-specific support to encourage and support Mark's efforts to learn the new job.

High direction and high work-specific support are the obvious supervisory behaviors that best respond to Mark's needs. At the same time, because Mark is highly motivated and anxious to learn, the supervisor should begin—on a limited basis—to provide personal and professional development support. Understanding that the majority of supervisory support is directed to helping the F-2 employee learn and master the skills needed to succeed on the job, including a limited amount of personal and professional development helps to send a motivating message. In essence, the supervisor's behavior demonstrates the organization's commitment to responding to the personal and professional needs of the employee.

This supervisory approach is called the S-2 approach. Graphed, the relationship looks as follows:

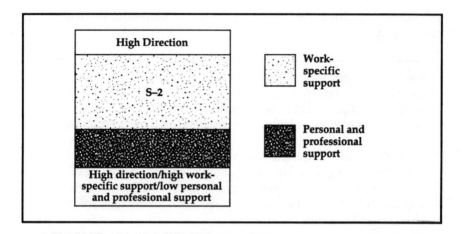

As you can see, the S-2 approach calls for high direction, high work-specific support, and a limited amount of personal and professional development support. It also responds directly to the supervisory needs of the F-2 employee.

Chapter 6 focuses exclusively on the F-2 employee. It reviews how employees become F-3 employees and how you can most effectively help an F-2 employee grow and mature into an F-4 employee.

The F-3 Employee

At training sessions on the Functional Management Model participants were asked which type of employee concerned them the most. A high percentage responded with F-3. F-3 employees are those with high ability and low motivation. They have the skills to succeed on the job but have lost their motivation.

Donna has worked in the home care industry for nearly 20 years. Previously, whe worked as a nurse at the local hospital. When she switched to home care, she found it a profession that was both challenging and exciting. She was good at what she did and won the agency's Award for Excellence five years ago.

Over the past few years, things began to change. While Donna shows up for work on time and always reaches the minimum productivity standards, she is clearly not excited or motivated to do the job. She has become the department's lowest performer; her lack of enthusiasm and involvement is affecting other members of the department.

Donna is a classic F-3 employee—high ability and low motivation. She was a high performer, but for whatever reason, has lost much of her enthusiasm and motivation. Some would call her burned out.

It is my experience that when supervisors make mistakes in supervising an employee, it is very often with an F-3 employee. Supervisors see that the employee is just barely getting by and lacks motivation. They want to ensure consistent productivity and increase the employee's motivation. What supervisors often do is fall prey to the belief that the best thing for the employee is to increase the training and work-specific support. Unfortunately, this is the wrong decision. F-3 employees do not lack skills or ability. They've come through in the past and are coming through now, though marginally. They don't need training; by giving them high direction you run the risk of degrading and demoralizing them. Can you imagine how a former high performer like Donna would feel if you tried to train her on medical procedures that she has practiced successfully for years?

All F-3 employees need is low direction, not a lot of support on how to do a job that they've been doing for nearly 20 years.

What F-3 employees like Donna need is personal and professional development support. The supervisor should explore and identify personal issues that are blocking Donna's former level of high performance. Don't overstep your boundaries; explore this area only to the degree that is profesionally and legally appropriate.

At the same time, by putting increased emphasis on providing higher levels of personal and professional development support, you can recapture Donna's interest and enthusiasm. What work barriers are in Donna's way? What new challenges or opportunities would interest Donna? What would help make the job more personally and professionally satisfying to Donna.

In short, the F-3 employee needs high personal and professional development support, and low direction and low work-specific support. Graphically, it looks as follows:

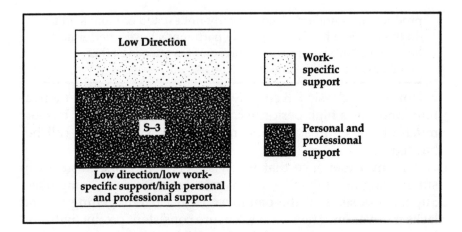

Notice the inverse relation between work-specific support and personal and professional development support. As the need to provide work-specific support decreases, that of personal and professional development support increases. Also, the graph makes it clear that when an employee is assessed as having high ability, the correct supervisory behavior is one that provides low direction. Chapter 7 will provide a thorough analysis and specific strategies for working with the F-3 employee.

The F-4 Employee

Managers love the F-4 employee. This employee has the knowledge and skills to succeed. Even better, F-4 employees are confident, enthusiastic, and highly motivated.

Anthony was the ideal employee. He started his career as an insurance broker and decided to move into management. Over the past 10 years he continued to progress and was appointed department head of the Claims Division two years ago.

Anthony loved his job. It was challenging and he learned a great deal. He liked working for a company that respected its employees. One of the best things about the company was that if you were self-motivated and had a good supervisor, it let you test out new procedures or programs. This made the organization a very positive, exciting place to work.

Anthony is a classic F-4 employee—high ability and high motivation. On the surface, he is an employee who might seem easy to supervise. But don't jump to that conclusion too quickly.

A question that most managers ask when reflecting on their F-4 employees is, "How do I keep them committed and motivated, and ensure that they don't become bored?" The answer lies in knowing the appropriate balance of supervisory behaviors—a logic that makes sense.

First, the F-4 employee obviously does not need high levels of training and direction. He already knows how to do the job. Because most jobs are interrelated and new information is always being generated, a limited amount of information sharing and coordination is always warranted. Low direction is therefore needed.

However, minimal work-specific support is still warranted because even your highest performers need some positive feedback. While this feedback is not directed at reassuring F-4 employees in learning a job, it does recognize their continued contribution.

The real focus and challenge for Anthony's supervisor is in identifying and providing him with personal and professional development support that responds directly to his personal and professional needs. The supervisor should therefore work with Anthony to explore ways to provide him with opportunities to grow personally and professionally.

This approach to supervision is called the S-4 supervisory approach. On a graph, the last of the three supervisory behaviors looks as follows:

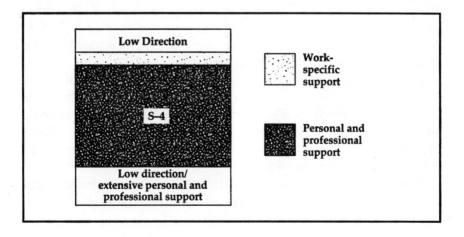

Developing appropriate personal and professional development support for specific employees is time consuming, yet critically important. The challenge is to reach a joint agreement with the employee on a manageable range of personal and professional efforts that the employee values. Once done, you've taken a giant step toward maintaining your subordinate at the F-4 level. (See Chapter 9 for a detailed discussion of strategies and options concerning F-4 employees.)

The graph shows that the S-4 supervisory approach calls for low direction, minimal work-specific support, and extensive personal and professional development support.

INTEGRATING THE FOUR SUPERVISORY APPROACHES

While each of the four supervisory approaches calls for different strategies and approaches to supervising specific employees, they share a common factor: They utilize the three major supervisory behaviors—direction, work-specific support, and personal and professional development support.

It is important to note that although each supervisory approach calls for different combinations and degrees of supervisory behaviors, all four share in utilization of these behaviors. By acknowledging that the three behaviors are the foundation for all four approaches, managers know what they need to focus on and what they need to learn. As they become more proficient in the three behaviors, they become more effective in the four approaches. And the more effective they are in using the four approaches, the more effective they will be as supervisors.

One of the greatest weaknesses of managers is their failure to recognize the skills they need to learn to use any one of the three supervisory behaviors. If you don't know what is necessary to be successful, how can you ever improve? So it goes to say that a manager cannot use the three supervisory behaviors successfully if he or she is unaware of them.

The components shared by each of the four supervisory approaches are readily seen in a single, comprehensive chart.

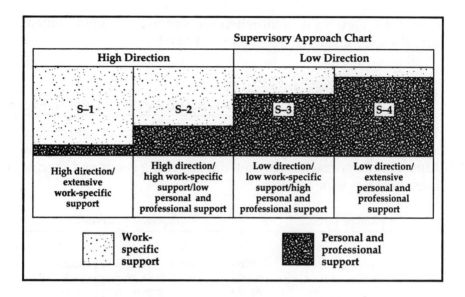

The relationships, particularly between work-specific support and personal and professional development support, become much clearer. You can see that as the need for work-specific support decreases, the need for personal and professional support increases. From a supervisory perspective, this makes sense.

The manager should use the S-1 and S-2 supervisory approaches to respond to employees who need skills and knowledge essential to successfully functioning on the job. The graph shows that high direction and work-specific support are needed.

The S-3 and S-4 supervisory approaches are used when responding to employees who already know how to do the job. The graph shows that low direction is needed. At the same time, personal and professional development support increases in order to maintain or reenergize the employee toward optimal performance.

Standing alone, the chart provides a clear perspective on the use of the three supervisory behaviors in the four supervisory approaches.

When integrated with the Functional Level Chart, the chart does one other very important thing: it provides an understandable, total view of a comprehensive supervisory management model—the Functional Management Model.

CREATING THE TOTAL SUPERVISORY MODEL

The direct relationship between functional levels and supervisory approaches should be apparent to you at this point. The various supervisory approaches respond directly to the needs and specific functional levels of employees.

Functional Level		Supervisory Approach
F-1 level employee	needs	S-1 supervisory approach
F-2 level employee	needs	S-2 supervisory approach
F-3 level employee	needs	S-3 supervisory approach
F-4 level employee	needs	S-4 supervisory approach

The nice thing about all this is that the relationship makes sense. It provides managers with clear guidelines for developing strategies to more effectively supervise and respond to their employees' needs. Most important, it's flexible and capable of responding to employees functioning at various levels. The relationship between functional levels and supervisory approaches can be clearly understood (see the Functional Management Model chart).

The full Functional Management Model combines material illustrated in the Functional Level and Supervisory Approach charts into a highly practical graphic that shows the relationship between them. The Functional Management Model provides supervisors with a clear perspective on how to respond to any employee. The flexibility of the model allows supervisory approaches to be adjusted as an employee moves from one functional level to another. By maintaining a consistent response to employees at specific functional levels, the model ensures the supervisor's internal integrity and predictability.

The common language of the Functional Management Model allows supervisors to communicate quickly to their superiors,

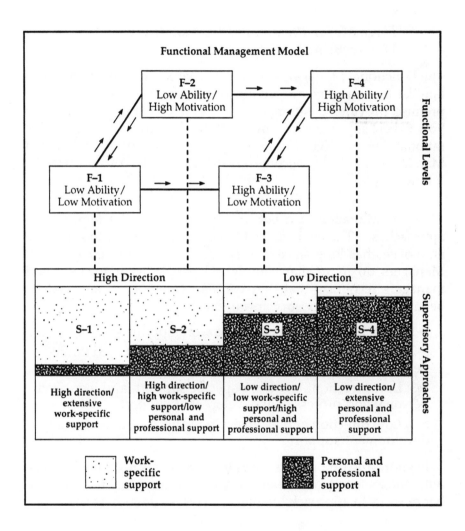

Functional Management Model

other supervisors, and even employees. When you say that an employee is functioning at an F-2 level, your colleagues and superiors know what you are dealing with. You can share ideas on how to respond to the problems of an employee.

Finally, the Functional Management Model allows you—in three easy steps—to devise effective supervision strategies. This is one of the real strengths of the model.

Three Major Premises of the Functional Management Model

The Functional Management Model is based on three premises—familiar to managers—based on solid research and practice. Each premise provides a rational, logical foundation for determining how to best supervise employees. If the premise makes sense, the rationale, responsiveness, and appropriateness of the Functional Management Model become crystal clear. The three premises follow.

1. Managers use not one but a number of supervisory approaches. The old logic that there is only one way to supervise employees has long since lost its hold on modern management. Managers do more than simply tell people what to do. Good managers recognize that they can use a number of supervisory behaviors and supervisory approaches.

S-1: High direction and extensive work-specific support

S-2: High direction, high work-specific support, and limited personal and professional development support

S-3: Low direction, low work-specific support, and increased personal and professional development support

S-4: Low direction and extensive personal and professional development support

In short, the first premise says that managers need not be stuck with one answer to all supervisory challenges. They have a number of ways to approach the matter. This is common sense.

2. Employees do not function at the same levels of skill and motivation. Supervisors know that all of their employees are not the same. Even employees with the same background may function at different levels. As you know, when the two key variables, ability and motivation, are put together, four types of employees emerge who can be found in almost any workplace:

F-1: Low Ability/Low Motivation

F-2: Low Ability/High Motivation

F-3: High Ability/Low Motivation

F-4: High Ability/High Motivation

By recognizing this premise, you will know that all employees cannot and should not be supervised and supported in the same manner. Like the first premise, this too is common sense.

3. Achieving optimal supervision by adjusting the approach to the employee's functional level.   The best supervisory approach is one that responds to the supervisory needs and functional level of the employee. If you know why an employee is functioning at a certain functional level, you have the basic rationale for knowing what supervisory approach will be most responsive to the needs of that employee. Doesn't this premise also sound like common sense?

How to Apply the Functional Management Model

The next four chapters will outline in detail how to apply the model effectively when supervising each of the four functional levels of employees. Each chapter contains an implied five-step approach to determine and apply the model. It is important to identify the five general steps.

1. **Assess the functional level of the employee.** Expect to spend a good deal of time analyzing the employee's abilities and motivation. Take your time and do it right.

First, look at the employee's ability level. Can this employee do the job? What facts and examples verify your conclusion? Are you confident about your conclusion? Is there anything else you could do to check it out? Is there anyone you can talk to? Be sure you have the facts and examples to substantiate your position.

Next, assess the employee's motivational level. Is it high or low? How do you know? What examples substantiate your position? Are you looking at more than one example? Motivation should be measured over time and not in a one-shot session. Review the employee's longer term performance before making a final decision.

One suggestion—document! Carefully document the examples that substantiate your position on the employee's ability and motivation. This could make your effort much easier later.

For the most part, once you have accurately assessed the functional level of employees, you will discover that they tend to stay at that level for a period of time. Ideally, your F-4 employee will be at the F-4 level for a long time and employees at other levels only long enough to learn what they need in order to become F-4 employees.

2. **Define your employee's supervisory needs and your supervisory goals.** Once you have a sense of the employees' functional level, their supervisory needs and your goals become more apparent.

You might determine that an F-2 employee needs specific training to learn the skills to succeed on the job. At the same time, your supervisory goal will be to continue to keep the employee enthusiastic and motivated about the job. The key to this step is to ensure consistency between your assessment of an employee's supervisory needs and his or her functional level.

Notice one thing: so far, all your efforts have been done primarily in isolation. What happens if your employees don't agree with your assessment of their functional level? How do you get them involved? That's where step three comes in.

3. **Clarify your assessment and goals with the employee.** Most supervisors dread this step. Tell the employee what your honest assessment of his or her functional level is and how you propose to supervise and support the employee.

Remember how you were cautioned to document and substantiate your position? Well, if you did it right this step won't be a problem. If you were hasty, you could be in trouble.

This step is important because if you and your employee are in agreement, what the employee wants you have to give. Both parties must be aware of how the supervisor perceives the employee and how the supervisor will then manage the employee.

Two final points. During the initial meeting, it is possible that the employee will disagree with the supervisor's assessment and will present a compelling argument to the contrary. If the supervisor accepts the employee's argument, then it is absolutely appropriate for the assessment and supervisory goals to be adjusted.

Second, if the supervisor and employee do not agree, the final decision rests with the supervisor. There is no confusion over this. The supervisor is responsible for the work of the unit and for making the final determination. The supervisor must make the final assessment known to the employee. No one ever said being a supervisor was easy.

4. **Determine the supervisory approach that best responds to the functional level.** The Functional Management Model provides you with a solid rationale to define the best approach to use for responding to the supervisory needs of employees at specific functional levels.

The rationale makes sense. It calls for using one of four supervisory approaches to provide employees at specific functional levels with the optimal balance of directive behavior, work-specific support, and personal and professional development support.

When applying the Functional Management Model, always look at the employee's ability level. If you are not sure the employee has the skills to do the job, it is better to err on the side of caution and assume that he or she may not have the skills. This ensures that you provide the employee with higher levels of direction and work-specific support.

If later you discover that you are wrong—that the employee does have the skills needed to do the job—you can reassess the employee's functional level and provide less direction and work-specific support, and more personal and professional development support. By playing it safe, you don't run the risk of jeopardizing the efforts of your department.

5. **Apply the appropriate supervisory approach and document and monitor the results.** Apply the approach in a manner that responds to the supervisory needs of the employee.

Employees new to the job or who are struggling with it need the supervisor to be more directive. They depend on you to define what they need to succeed. Despite plenty of supportive dialog between you and the employee, you will obviously be making more of the decisions concerning the training and development of the employee. Higher performers should have more input into the types of personal and professional development support they need. By involving them in the supervisory process, you reinforce the organization's recognition of their work maturity and ability to do the job.

All good supervisors monitor their efforts and the effects of their efforts. Ongoing monitoring ensures that the supervisor is aware of the needs of the employee.

Dealing With Your Realities

Knowing the Functional Management Model is only half of the formula for success. The other half is knowing how to apply the model. What is the best way to apply the model with your F-1 employees? What happens if they don't change? How do you know the training needs of your F-2 employees? Should you focus on the job or encourage their personal and professional development? What about your F-3 employees? How do you remotivate them? What happens if they stay unmotivated and begin affecting the morale of other members of your department? How do you keep F-4 employees committed and motivated? How can you use their talents and high levels of motivation most effectively?

There are lots of questions that need to be answered in applying the model. The good news is that it provides clear answers to help you with all four levels of employees. The next four chapters explore strategies that are effective for specific functional levels and review how employees got to a specific level. You will see what works and what doesn't. And you will find numerous options for approaching and supervising specific staff.

Chapter Six

The Struggling Employee
The F-1 Employee: Low Ability/Low Motivation

B efore every training session on the Functional Management Model, participants are asked to describe the type of employee who frustrates them most. Who do you think they name?—the F-1 employee. You realize that for many supervisors the F-1 employee is incredibly frustrating.

My experience is that F-1 employees cause more complaints and consternation than employees at any other level. Remember, an F-1 employee lacks both the ability to do the job in a timely and qualitative manner and the drive and motivation to consistently get the job done. Supervisors often see them as lazy and apathetic, and often not very bright. Many feel that the F-1 employee is born unmotivated and uncaring.

As you can see from the Functional Level Chart, F-1 employees have farther to go than F-2 and F-3 employees to become F-4 employees. Not only do they need to become motivated and driven to do the job, but also they must learn the skills required to succeed. It is no wonder that supervisors view them as "struggling employees."

The first thing I try to do is dispel these misperceptions about F-1 employees. The vast majority of F-1 employees do not want to be F-1 employees. Many are embarrassed. They know they lack the necessary skills and the confidence or enthusiasm to be self-motivated. Most realize how they are being perceived and don't like it. Most would prefer to be more successful.

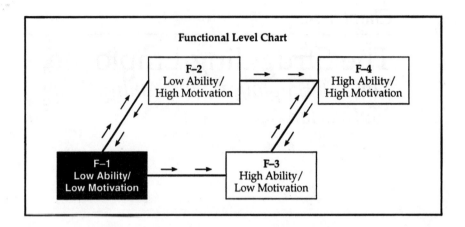

UNDERSTANDING THE F-1 EMPLOYEE

Think about what it means to be an F-1 employee. They are basically failing at work. They know it, they know you know it, and they realize that their colleagues know it. Even those in the most protected jobs fear that they could someday run into problems and be out of work.

Before you, as a supervisor, can deal effectively with an F-1 employee, it is helpful to review how an employee arrives at that functional level. While no two people are alike or share the same life experiences, it does appear that people become F-1 employees by three common ways. These ways became apparent from feedback and discussions with participants in the workshops and from meetings with managers at all levels in public and private organizations.

1. Employees fail to learn the skills to succeed on the job. A newly hired employee normally comes to the job pleased to have been hired. Most new employees are highly motivated and want to succeed. Aren't most new employees classic F-2 employees?

Well, that's where the problem begins for many eventual F-1 employees. They come to the job committed and motivated, ready to learn and succeed, looking forward to the challenges and opportunities. And then they fail to learn the skills they need to succeed. Each day they are unable to do all that is required of them in a timely and qualitative manner. Instead of experiencing success, they experience failure.

As the days go on, they become more and more disillusioned. Their self-esteem suffers. As they continue to fail to learn, they become less and less motivated. It's hard to be motivated when you constantly experience failure. Then slowly—faster for those with lower self-esteem —they give up and eventually evolve to an F-1 level. What is their goal at this stage? Normally, survival. They do what they can to avoid getting fired.

You ask, "How and why did they fail to learn the skills? " First, they may have been hired into a position that was beyond them. They may have lacked the fundamental knowledge base needed for learning new skills.

Learning is a cumulative process. Consider how a child acquires language. First, the child babbles. Next the child begins to use simple words. Then the child can combine words. Soon the child speaks in simple sentences. Sentences gradually become longer and more complex and begin to be combined with other sentences. Eventually the child is completely articulate.

A child who never learned those first simple words would never have advanced to a more complex language. Likewise, the F-1 worker who has not acquired the basic skills that serve as the foundation on which to build the required skills will never succeed on the job.

There is a second way an employee may regress from an F-2 to an F-1 level. An F-2 employee may have the basic knowledge needed to learn new skills and be ready and eager to learn. Then something happens, or we should say doesn't happen. The supervisor either fails to provide the necessary training and support or provides training that is beyond the capacity of the employee. For either reason, the employee does not learn the skills, loses confidence and motivation, and slowly sinks into the F-1 function level.

And now the painful news! If your F-1 employee has regressed from the F-2 level, this usually has not come about through any fault of the employee. Looking for someone to blame? You probably need look no further than your own mirror.

Let's face it, the employee did not want this to happen in either scenario. With the first F-1 employee, you probably failed to recruit, screen, and hire the appropriate person for the job. With the second, you failed to provide the right levels of training and support. Either way, the employee who has dropped from the F-2 level to the F-1 level can't make you feel very good. Fortunately, as you will see in Chapter 7, it doesn't have to happen.

2. Employees who are the victims of downsizing and organizational shuffling. Public and private organizations are now going through incredible structural and staffing changes. Flatten the organization. Lean and mean. Eliminate levels. These are the battle cries of today's organizations.

Erase all the buzz phrases and rhetoric, and what does this mean? It means that many employees who were hired and trained to do a certain job suddenly found themselves shuffled off to a totally new job or, worse, terminated.

The employees who were transferred to new jobs because they had seniority or were protected by a union contract often felt lucky. Maybe they were, but many paid a price for this "luck." Many found themselves in jobs for which they had no training. Worse, they often found themselves in jobs in which they never had any interest.

In a large state mental health agency, cutbacks in state government resulted in layoffs and reassignments of staff. One senior member of the Licensing Department—a department responsible for monitoring programs and regulations—was reassigned. Because he had a master's degree he was reassigned to a mental health clinic, and there into the sole position available— therapist. Although he was trained as a therapist, he had never done a single hour of counseling. He felt that he was forced into the position.

For employees who find themselves pulled from the familiarity of their existing job and established relationships, the trauma of the changes can be overwhelming. When they find themselves in jobs that they were never trained to do, the trauma can become even worse.

Unfortunately, transferred or reassigned employees often start out as F-1 employees because they are there by choice. And if they have no inclination or aptitude for the job, they often get stuck at the F-1 level.

3. Modernization of the employee's department. Times are changing rapidly. Fax machines. Beepers. Car phones. Voice mail. Teleconferencing. The changes have a profound effect on how you do business. When I completed my doctorate at the University of Massachusetts in 1983, I would guess that less than half of those submitting dissertations at that time had them prepared on a computer. Today you would be hard-pressed to find even one doctoral candidate who does not do everything on the computer.

The rapid change in technoloogy in the office is matched by changes on the shop floor, on the farm, and in services industries. While these changes are impressive, for some of the workers who are living through them they have proved overwhelming. Employees may have been incredibly successful at their jobs prior to technological changes—F-4 employees perhaps—but now they find themselves unable to learn the new technology. Younger employees seem to be catching on quicker. For others, the harder they try, the worse it gets. Instead of being looked up to by their colleagues, they realize that they are being looked over.

As they become less confident about using the new technology, they lose their enthusiasm and motivation. It's got to be pretty demoralizing for them to be unable to do a job at which they previously excelled. So, lacking the ability to do the job in a timely and qualitative manner, and subsequently losing their drive and motivation, these employees slip to the F-1 level.

How is it possible for F-4 employees to regress to the F-1 Level? Once they learn the skills, don't they always have them? True, but remember: Functional levels are based on an assessment of a person in a specific job. If you change the job—changing the technology and the way things are done changes the job—then you have to reassess the Functional Level of the employee in the new job. And you have to ask the same questions. Do they have the skills (the new skills with the new technology) and are they motivated?

When a department undergoes a significant technological change that substantially redefines how employees do their job, employees must obviously learn new skills. While learning the new skills, F-4 employees function at the F-2 level. If the skills are learned successfully, they evolve to an F-4 level. If they don't, and if they slowly lose their motivation and enthusiasm, you eventually will have demoralized, depressed F-1 employees.

All changes don't have to be technological. With the emergence of total quality management as a guiding philosophy for managing employees in contemporary organizations, staff at all levels are asked to become active participants in shaping and influencing the future of their companies. Midmanagers are asked to be less autocratic and more facilitative in their interaction with staff. Managers are strongly encouraged to push for employee participation and involvement.

For some managers, the need to shift from directive to a more participatory form of leadership is extremely difficult. They lack much of the knowledge and many of the skills needed to be empowering managers. They find that the challenges and demands brought about by new management philosophies may be just as overwhelming and problematic as the changes caused by the introduction of new technologies.

Accepting the Reality of Change

At no point am I suggesting that organizations avoid upgrading their operations or introducing new technology for fear employees will be required to learn new skills or supervisors new ways of management. To resist change is to doom your organization to obsolescence.

What I *am* suggesting is that change will affect the functional levels of employees; they will need to learn new skills. Responsible organizations and supervisors also must recognize what change means to employees—even high functioning employees —and initiate strategies to help employees successfully accept and adapt to the changes.

CAN AN F-1 EMPLOYEE BE HELPED?

Many managers give up on those employees they believe are functioning at the F-1 level. They see them as hopeless, unable and unwilling to change. This is not true!

Karl Albrecht is a leader in the customer service and total quality service movement. With Ron Zemke, he wrote *Service America,* which called for all industries to make a total commitment to providing exceptional services to customers of the organization.[1] In a later book, *The Only Thing that Matters*, Albrecht emphasizes the importance of empowering and involving staff in creating exceptional organizations. He believes that with the right leadership, all employees can be re-energized and made significant members of an organization.

> Some of the hardest employees to win over are those suffering from terminal cases of burnout. This may be the result of downsizings, reorganizations, buyouts, mergers, or the unique pressures of the industry itself. And yet, even these people can usually find their way back to working with energy and commitment if their leaders understand their needs and know how to empower them.[2]

Albrecht's point is valid. These employees can be helped to learn and grow beyond their F-1 level. They can even become your future F-4 employees. However, Albrecht warns this can come about only if managers understand employee needs and know how to act upon them.

THE F-1 EMPLOYEE: A CASE STUDY

You know what an F-1 employee is and some of the ways that a person becomes one. What you really need to know, however, is how to supervise F-1 employees most effectively. How can you help them learn the skills needed to succeed? How can you help them increase their motivation?

Five steps provide you with a systematic way to approach employees. The five steps are the same steps used in supervising any employee. The title of this section could be, "Five Steps to Effectively Supervise All Employees." What changes from one functional level to the next is what you do within each step. This approach takes full advantage of the Functional Management Model and ensures that all your supervisory strategies are targeted to the functional level of the employee.

In this chapter and subsequent chapters on supervising F-2, F-3 and F-4 employees, case studies will be used to clarify your understanding of the Functional Management Model and of the best means of supervising each type of employee.

As you review the five steps in using the Functional Management Model, reflect back on the case study and suggest specific strategies for each step. In this way, the practical aspects of the model will become more apparent.

One note of caution: none of the strategies outlined is suggested as the only way to approach each step. In supervision, there is never only one way. What is suggested are strategies that are clearly appropriate and responsible to the realities you will deal with. You may feel that a different set of strategies would be more responsive. That's okay. As long as you take full advantage of the Functional Management Model, the individual strategies you develop within each step may be equally appropriate. If you think new strategies are warranted, don't be afraid to try them to help your employees.

"I've had it," said Dan. "Everything I do is wrong. I hate coming to work. I hate being a failure. And I hate disappointing you and my colleagues. Why did this have to happen?" he asked his supervisor.

Dan had worked in the insurance agency for the past 11 years. He had enjoyed the company and the people with whom he worked. He had steadily moved up in the organization. Three years ago he was named senior auditor in the Claims Department. He loved the job and was clearly very good at it.

Nine months ago, his company was bought out by one of the nation's largest insurance companies. At first, there were few changes, but slowly a number of significant changes took place. The most devastating change for Dan was the consolidation of his function into a single Audit Department in the new company's main office. Dan was given the option of transferring to the main office in a different state or staying where he was but in a different job. He opted to stay.

Dan was transferred to the Actuarial Department because of his fiscal and mathematics background. There was much to learn: new procedures, new forms, new regulations, and a new computer system.

Initially Dan was committed to making the best of his new position. Unfortunately, he found the new job with its regulations and procedures difficult to learn. He couldn't master many of the expectations of the job. The more he tried, the more he failed. It was clear to Dan's supervisor that he did not possess the knowledge and skills needed to succeed. He also clearly lacked the enthusiasm and motivation needed to learn the skills. What should his supervisor do?

In discussing how to deal with Dan, it is important to bear in mind that every strategy for every employee must be individually defined. In addition, "canned" approaches don't work. They are often a disservice to you and to your employees because supervisors tend to focus more on the approach than on the supervisory needs of the employee.

APPLYING THE FUNCTIONAL MANAGEMENT MODEL

Through the Functional Management Model, you always focus on the supervisory needs of the employee first; then you develop specific strategies that use the appropriate supervisory approach. Let's review the five steps to use the Functional Management Model effectively:

Step 1: Assess the Functional Level of the Employee

The essence of the Functional Management Model is knowing how an employee is functioning and adjusting your supervisory approach to the functional level and supervisory needs of the employee. Accurately assessing the employee's functional level is essential to successfully supervising any employee.

Don't take this step too lightly. Don't quickly choose a functional level and move on. The key to the Functional Management Model lies in targeting the forms of supervisory support to the functional level of the employee. If you make a mistake on this step, subsequent steps will become increasingly inappropriate.

To effectively assess an employee's functional level, you need to spend some time reflecting on what you know about the employee. More important, you must document behaviors that support your assessment. This will come in handy during step two.

As you look at the ability level of the employee, what do you observe? What specific skills or knowledge does the F-1 employee seem to lack? What concrete examples support this assessment? If challenged, can you provide verifiable documentation to support your assessment?

How do you assess the employee's motivational level? What concrete examples can you identify? You will soon find that motivation is harder to measure. Unlike skills that can be tested, motivation is more amorphous.

Among the things to look at are the employee's initiative and self-confidence. Are employees self-initiating or do they require your direction and encouragement to perform the task? Can you rely on them to come through or do you have to push them? Are they confident or are they unsure and hesitant?

What concrete examples support your contention that the F-1 employee has low motivation? Again, the more concrete you can be, the easier it will be for you to accurately determine the employee's functional level.

When you feel you have made a thorough analysis of how the employee is functioning on his or her present job, you are ready to determine the functional level. Obviously, if you feel the employee lacks both ability and motivation, you have identified your classic F-1 employee.

It didn't take Dan's supervisor long to assess and verify Dan's functional level. Dan was having difficulty doing certain aspects of the job. Dan himself stated that he couldn't seem to learn certain procedures.

It was also clear to the supervisor that Dan had low motivation. He never initiated anything. He always required tight supervision. If the supervisor wasn't there, quite likely Dan would not get much work done. Dan was clearly an F-1 employee.

Dan's supervisor had successfully completed the first step in the supervisory process; he had assessed Dan's functional level and had established clear documentation that supported and verified his position. He was now ready for step two.

Step 2: Define Employees' Needs and Your Supervisory Goals

You must do one thing before you start any supervisory efforts with an F-1 employee or any level of employee: You must have a clear sense of what you are trying to accomplish.

First, consider what you know about the F-1 employee. If you accurately assessed his or her functional level, you know the employee lacks the knowledge and skills to do the job. If the F-1 employee could not perform in a job and also lacks the confidence for reliably moving ahead, it stands to reason that this person's motivation and self-esteem in relation to the job is low.

When you review the Functional Level component of the Functional Management Model chart (presented earlier), it is apparent that your ultimate goal is to improve the ability and motivation of the F-1 employee.

Lack of motivation is sometimes harder to recognize than lack of ability. For example, managers invariably make statements like, "Even though she is an F-1 employee, she doesn't act as if she lacks confidence or feels bad about herself in relation to the job." This is certainly true of many employees.

Since childhood many people were taught to hide their emotions. You probably remember hearing statements like, "Nobody likes a cry baby." "Big boys [or girls] don't cry." "Be tough." "Emotions are a sign of weakness." The implied message for children is don't let people see how you feel.

As adults, many if not most of your F-1 employees live and work by the same axiom: Don't let people see how you feel. It is important for you as their supervisor to be aware of the feelings that go along with poor performance. The more sensitive you are to their feelings, the greater the probability that you will be able to successfully support and supervise employees.

Now you have a good sense of what their supervisory needs are and you can define your supervisory goals.

With F-1 employees, you often have four specific supervisory goals.

1. Help employees learn the skills to succeed.   When you have finished reading this book and are done thinking about process and the needs of your employees, one fact that remains is that all employees must have the skills to succeed. You must provide F-1 employees with training opportunities—either directly or by access to the appropriate resources—that give them these skills.

2. Encourage employees to talk about job concerns. Employees are having trouble learning the job. They are experiencing failure. They know they are not doing well. Rather than ignoring the employees, encourage them to talk about their concerns. The more you know about their needs and concerns, the easier it will be for you to come up with strategies to help. For struggling employees, the chance to honestly discuss their fears, concerns, and frustrations with the supervisor can be a powerful step toward becoming more open to changing their behavior.

3. Task-related feedback. You know that your F-1 employees are struggling because they lack the skills to do the job. One of the key things that these employees need is direct feedback on how they are doing. It is critical for a supervisor to allow time and develop the means to provide them with extensive positive and corrective feedback—positive feedback to reinforce their gains and constructive feedback to correct mistakes.

4. Provide extensive encouragement and support. You know that F-1 employees don't feel good about their job performance. Low ability and motivational levels make this clear. As their supervisor, you must reinforce their self-esteem and make them feel better about their accomplishments. This doesn't mean false praise, which is worse than no praise because they know it's not true.

Rather, recognize that F-1 employees suffer the feelings associated with lack of success, lack of recognition, and lack of feeling supported and valued. Appropriate encouragement, support, and work-related feedback will go a long way toward rebuilding their confidence and motivation.

For Dan, the supervisor's goals were clear. She needed to work with Dan to identify the specific new skills that he needed to learn. She needed either to provide those skills or make them available to Dan. She needed to monitor Dan closely and provide ongoing feedback on his progress. Finally, she needed to help Dan feel supported and appreciated as he struggled to improve his performance.

In many ways, Dan was lucky. His supervisor realized how difficult it must have been for Dan to go through the job changes he was forced into, and she was willing to do what she could to help Dan succeed.

With a clear understanding of what your supervisory goals are, you are now ready to sit down with your employees and begin the process of helping them improve their overall performance level. The third step of this process is to provide your employees with an honest assessment of how you view their level of functioning. Then you will initiate specific supervisory strategies and begin monitoring their performances.

Step 3: Clarify Your Assessment with F-1 Employees

Employees can be frustrated a great deal when they feel that their supervisor is not giving appropriate supervision and support. It is particularly frustrating when employees feel confident, yet find themselves treated as if they lacked the skills to do the job or need to be continually watched.

It is critical that both you and your employees have a clear understanding of what you believe to be their functional level. Most employees want to know. In session after session, when employees were asked, "If you know that your supervisor has determined your functional level, would you want to know what that assessment is?" no less than 90 percent of participants said yes.

From a supervisory perspective, you cannot expect to help employees unless you are totally honest. That means that you will let them know your perception of their ability and motivation levels.

For those organizations that have adopted the Functional Management Model companywide, you must tell the employee that it is your assessment that he or she is functioning at an F-1 level. Use the langauge of the model. Employees who have been taught the model and know its language will know exactly what you mean.

If an employee is not familiar with the model, focus on the two functional criteria—ability and motivation—and relate that you believe the employee is exhibiting low performances in both.

Either way, it is critical that you document your position. If you say the employee is low in ability, you must have concrete examples to support your position. Don't tell the employee that it is your *feeling* or impression. If you believe it and say it, you must prove it.

Dan's supervisor was very clear with Dan. She told him that she knew he was really struggling and clearly having difficulty with certain parts of the job. She recognized that he had initially tried to learn the new skills but she had to point out that he was currently showing little initiative and required a lot of monitoring and encouragement to get the job done.

Dan at first denied he was struggling. But when his supervisor provided a number of concrete examples, he had to admit that things weren't easy and that he was having trouble keeping up with his colleagues. While he had difficulty accepting that he was at an F-1 level, he did agree that the supervisor had raised legitimate questions about his overall ability and motivation.

It should be no surprise that Dan had difficulty acknowledging that he had problems with ability and motivation. While most employees recognize their shortcomings, they often play down the seriousness of the situation. Because F-1 employees are really in trouble—how long do you want to keep employees low in both ability and motivation?—it is essential that they understand the seriousness of their situation. Verifiable documentation is probably most important with F-1 employees. Documentation is a time-consuming step that cannot be glossed over or ignored.

Be prepared for emotional responses. What makes this step so emotionally difficult for employees is that you have to tell them things that they don't want to hear. No one wants to be viewed as a person who lacks the skills to do a job or who isn't motivated. A person feels threatened hearing these things. It hurts. The implied message is, "You are not making the grade and your performance must improve." The key point to this step is ensuring that employees know how they are functioning. Your honesty sets the groundwork for helping them to improve their performance.

This is not an easy meeting. You are, in essence, telling an employee that the employee is not making the grade, is failing, and is not pulling his or her weight. Your meeting is probably going to be emotional—painful for both you and the employee. It is not uncommon for an employee to respond emotionally with anger, tears, prolonged silence, or denial. These are a few of the reactions you might experience.

Expect this to happen and be prepared. Listen to the reaction to your assessment. Allow the employee to vent, within reason. But make sure you bring the conversation back to the verifiable facts that support your position. Don't get defensive. Be firm. This is a difficult part of the process but one for which you need to be prepared.

Affirm your belief in and commitment to the employee. As kind and gentle as you might have been, you've just given the employee some pretty disturbing information about failure on the job. How do you think the employee feels? How would you feel?

The challenge now is to move from the negative to the positive, from focusing on the employee's weaknesses and failures to focusing on strengths and potential. To make it, the F-1 employee is going to need all the help and support that you can give.

Point out the employee's strengths and areas of success. Focus on positive traits and characteristics. Most important, talk about why you feel the employee can succeed.

Step 4: Develop and Initiate Specific Supervisory Approach

Step three discussed what you are going to do to improve an F-1 employee's ability and motivation. Step four talks about how you are going to do it. Supervisory goals and behaviors will be the same from industry to industry, but the specific strategies that you use and what you focus on will differ. For example, the focus of a supervisor of an F-1 employee in an insurance company is quite different from that in a retail store, an assembly plant, or a state agency. But in general, you know that F-1 employees require an S-1 supervisory approach: high direction and extensive work-specific support. Let's take a more detailed look at both.

1. Providing high direction.   If you say that a person is an F-1 employee, you clearly state that he or she has low ability. Therefore you must be very clear and direct in providing support and training. It is not enough that you prepared for the supervisory meeting by documenting the employee's knowledge and skill deficiencies. You must also be prepared by determining how to provide the employee with the training needed to succeed on the job.

As you follow these steps, don't misunderstand the role of feedback and support. This isn't something you wait until step four to provide. Feedback and support aren't scheduled the same way as training. You must not say, "Aha, it's three o'clock—time to say something positive to Dan!"

Instead you need to provide F-1 employees with either positive or constructive feedback (I avoid using the word *negative*) at every possible opportunity: When you outline their training schedule, when you see them trying on the job, when you see them struggling, and when you see them doing something wrong. Or right— don't avoid giving them constructive feedback. Your challenge is to find opportunities to be aware of their efforts and to provide them with continued support.

The latter will include providing on-the-job training, providing mentors, sending them to seminars or training sessions, and requiring things to read or study. You need to know exactly what you will do to ensure that the employee gets the necessary training to succeed on the job.

Training is not an area in which to be vague. How are you going to ensure that an employee gets it? When will it be provided? Where? How? By whom? If money is needed, who will pay for it?

Employees should walk away from the meeting knowing exactly how they are going to get the training they need. They should have a specific schedule and training outline, know how long it will take, and what they are expected to know when it is completed. Supervisors should be providing employees with a training plan and schedule that will enable them to learn what is necessary in order to overcome their deficits.

2. Provide intensive work-specific support.   The second supervisory behavior needed with the S-1 approach is work-specific support.

After spending nearly three hours working with Dan to identify areas where he lacked specific skills, Dan's supervisor felt she had a clear grasp of what Dan needed to learn. Together they had reviewed all aspects of the job and jointly identified Dan's weaknesses.

It was now the supervisor's responsibility to identify how the training would be provided. She scheduled specific training sessions. She provided Dan with a mentor. She agreed to meet with him to go over specific tasks that he found particularly difficult. Finally, she established clear, measurable timelines for ensuring that each training was provided.

She didn't stop there. Throughout the training period, she made a special effort to be continually aware of Dan's progress. At every possible opportunity, she provided Dan not only with feedback on how he was doing but also with encouragement of his efforts and support of his progress.

Dan's supervisor clearly was not taking her responsibilities lightly. Like all good supervisors, she was making a commitment to doing whatever she could to help Dan succeed.

Once you have initiated your specific supervisory behavior strategies for F-1 or any employee, you must utilize one last step— monitoring, documenting, and refining your efforts—to increase the effectiveness of your supervision.

Step 5: Monitor, Document, and Refine Your Supervisory Efforts

If you tell employees that you expect improvements in their performance and specify exactly what you expect, then you need to make sure it happens. The worst thing you can do is tell employees that you expect a change and then forget about it or focus your attention elsewhere while the employees drift through the workweek.

Your credibility depends on employees knowing that what you say means something. If you tell F-1 employees that you expect improvement in skills and motivation on the job, then you have to monitor their performance to ensure it happens.

You do this first by scheduling regular review sessions during which you go over the employee's progress. Regularly scheduled review sessions are those that meet at an exact time, not some

vague time next week. They can be either special meetings or regularly scheduled supervisory sessions. Tuesday at 3:00. Wednesday at 10:30.

Next, document your assessment. Again, give your employees clear, concrete examples of how they are doing and what you have observed that makes you feel this way. If they are not progressing in a way that you expect, you need to tell them that.

Dan's supervisor clearly understood that she needed to tightly monitor Dan's progress. Initially that meant she would need to monitor Dan closely, meet with him often, and continually provide feedback and support. Dan needed to know that his supervisor was truly concerned about him and was serious about her commitment to support him and help him improve his performance.

Dan's supervisor scheduled two meetings a week for four weeks. The first was their regularly scheduled supervisory session at 2:00 P.M. Monday. The second, scheduled for Fridays at 1:00 P.M., was a special meeting. It was structured to review Dan's progress more thoroughly and to identify areas where Dan needed to try harder or where his supervisor needed to provide additional types of support.

The meetings allowed Dan's supervisor to monitor his progress. She was able to adjust how she was supporting him, make some changes, and add training in areas they had missed. Throughout the effort, supervision was supportive and responsive to Dan's needs.

This level of directive supervision meant a great deal to Dan. He felt supported. He felt his supervisor truly cared. And he felt he had the backup that could help him succeed. It was no wonder Dan's confidence came back and he slowly—sometimes very slowly—learned the skills to succeed.

Two points need to be emphasized. First, while it is true that an employee like Dan succeeded because he worked hard to improve his performance, it is equally true that Dan's supervisor deserves a great deal of credit. She clearly can take pride in knowing that Dan's success is a reflection of her efforts.

Second, in supervising and monitoring F-1 employees, it is important that you give them the chance to reflect on the changes that have taken place, including personal growth. For example, you could ask them:

- What were the most difficult aspects of the job to learn?
- Was there a particular point in time when you knew you were going to succeed?
- What types of support or guidance that I provided did you find helpful?
- What did you find not helpful?

The last two questions are particularly important. Not only can you gain new insights on how to be a more effective supervisor, you are *modeling openness* (demonstrating openness for the employee) and how to take constructive feedback. It also makes you come across as more approachable and more of a team player.

WHAT IF THE F-1 EMPLOYEE DOESN'T IMPROVE?

Like most supervisors, your immediate response to this question is probably: "Fire them!" You're almost right, but not quite. If you've done everything you can to help an F-1 employee improve and the employee still shows little or no change, something must be done. You cannot continue to tolerate an inadequate performance.

Employees who are not performing up to standard are not carrying their share of the work. They put stress on your department and on other members of your team. Because many of your employees are aware that substandard employees are not doing their fair share, they look to you to do something about it. Your credibility is on the line. What do you do?

First, and probably for the last time, review all that you've done with these employees. Did you give them a fair chance? Did you provide them with the necessary training? Did you encourage them? Did you provide meaningful and timely feedback and support? Did you do everything that could be reasonably expected to help these employees succeed?

Procedures for Terminating an F-1 Employee

If the answers are yes, then it's time to initiate termination procedures. Termination is different from firing in that termination is a process, while firing tends to be an abrupt action due to specific behavior or actions that violate strict organizational rules; if legally challenged, firing would be upheld. For obvious legal reasons, it is important that you check with legal counsel or verify your legal position before initiating any abrupt action. For legal reasons and to maintain fairness, a termination process is normally far more desirable.

Fortunately, you've already taken the first few steps to initiating a positive termination. Most organizations have established clear procedures for termination. Normally it is in writing. Check with your Human Resources or your supervisor before initiating termination procedures. A termination process typically involves five steps:

1. *Identification of performance problem by supervisor.* The supervisor identifies the performance problems and alerts the employee to the problems. This is a somewhat informal step and often is not considered as a part of the formal termination process. You've already done this in step three.

2. *Formal verbal warning.* The supervisor formally notifies the employee about serious performance problems. The supervisor verbally identifies expectations and measurable improvements, and schedules meetings to monitor progress. You've already done this in steps three, four, and five.

3. *Formal written warning.* If the employee does not improve his or her performance, the supervisor presents a written list of expectations and measurements. The supervisor also must tell the employee that if the necessary skills are not learned and he or she continues to demonstrate a lack of motivation, the employee will be terminated. Tight monitoring and formal meetings to review an employee's progress are then established. You've begun this in step five. The written part makes it formal and serious.

4. *Employee is placed on probation.* If the employee continues to demonstrate a lack of ability and motivation, the supervisor places the employee on formal probation. In essence, the formal probation says to an employee, "You've now burned all of your bridges. This is the last step. If you do not show marked improvement within my predefined timelines, you will no longer have this job." This step makes the gravity of the situation crystal clear to the employee. This step gives employees the option of quitting to

save face if they have come to the realization that they can't or don't want to do the job.

5. *Termination.* If the employee does not show marked improvement within predefined timelines and continues to exhibit unacceptable levels of performance, the employee must be terminated. It is critical that you are consistent and follow through on this threat. Your credibility and that of your organization are at stake.

Assuming you have been fair and have done everything possible to turn the employee around, you are simply upholding your end of an agreement. If the employee had improved, you would have followed through on your commitment to retain the employee. If not, you are simply following through with your commitment to terminate that employee.

A Supervisory Process that Works

The good thing about the five-step supervisory approach is that it works. It works as well for F-1 employees as it does for F-2, F-3, and F-4 level employees. The process is particularly appealing for two reasons. First, it is positive. It provides supervisors with every means and opportunity possible for helping employees. For F-1 employees, it provides the guidelines for helping employees gain the skills and motivation needed to succeed on the job.

Second, the process is realistic. It ensures that the supervisor generates the documentation and creates the foundation for initiating a positive termination for F-1 employees who are unable to meet performance standards.

Finally, the five steps provide supervisors with the means to help employees slowly and logically progress to an F-2 or F-3 level on their way to becoming F-4 employees.

HOW F-1 EMPLOYEES PROGRESS

It is true that F-1 employees are struggling. It is also true that they can make it and with the right kind of support can become your future F-4 employees. How do they progress?

The Functional Management Model chart presented earlier shows that F-1 employees can progress in one of two directions. They can slowly gain confidence and motivation and move up to an F-2 level. Later, as their skills increase, they can move on to an F-4 level. Or they could slowly learn the skills and move to a F-3 level; as their morale, confidence, and motivation increase, they move to the F-4 level.

It has been my experience that most employees progress by first gaining or regaining the confidence and motivation to learn and do the job. As their motivation increases, they try harder to learn the skills that they need to know.

Don't interpret this to mean that an F-1 employee first becomes motivated (F-2) and then learns the skills (F-4) or that they first learn the skills (F-3) and then become motivated (F-4). In reality, both skill development and motivation normally occur at the same time. As employees learn skills and experience success, they obviously feel good about themselves and become more motivated. Or as they become refocused and more motivated to learn the job, they try harder to learn the skills.

The reason F-1 employees tend to go to an F-2 or F-3 level rather than directly to F-4 is that most employees tend to show progress in either ability or motivation, but they don't show this progress in both at an equal rate.

Chapter Seven

The Motivated Learner
The F-2 Employee: Low Ability/High Motivation

I f someone were to ask supervisors what type of employee they most enjoy working with, they probably would say the F-2 employee. F-2 employees are motivated, eager to learn, and usually very positive. With the right type of supervisory support, they will evolve to become F-4 employees.

F-2 employees make work fun. They are receptive to change and usually willing to get involved in new efforts. They often volunteer to work on a project or help out other employees— particularly if they feel they will learn new skills along the way.

Because of their motivation and willingness to learn, F-2 employees have tremendous potential for becoming among your highest functioning employees, F-4 employees. But there is another, far less favorable, possibility. If F-2 employees don't learn the skills and knowledge needed on the job, they will eventually get discouraged (see Functional Level Chart). The longer they work without learning the necessary skills, the more discouraged they are likely to become. And it will only be a matter of time before they slowly sink to an F-1 functional level.

HOW WORKERS BECOME F-2 EMPLOYEES

It has been argued that the only true F-2 employees are those who are newly hired. While this is certainly true, a number of other types of employees also may be functioning at an F-2 level.

As a manager, the more you know about your employees, the greater your potential will be for successfully supervising them.

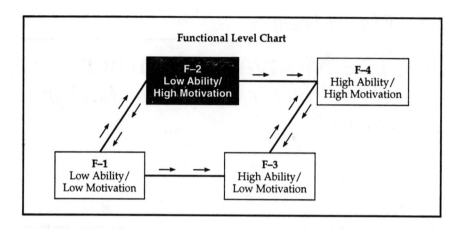

Knowing how they might have become F-2 employees is certainly knowledge that can help you become more sensitive to their needs and more effective in determining the best strategies for supervising and supporting them.

While there are certainly many paths that can lead an employee to function at the F-2 level, three ways are particularly prevalent.

1. The newly hired employee. There is no question that the highest percentage of F-2 employees are people recently hired into a position. New employees are generally people who are excited about getting the job. They applied for it because they wanted or needed it (or both). They are pleased that they got it and are anxious and motivated to succeed. Needless to say, employees don't apply for a job with the intent to fail.

At the same time, new employees normally lack some basic knowledge or skills related to the job—how much differs from one employee to another. Some employees may be moving into a totally new job, such as first-time employees who recently graduated from school. Others may be seasoned veterans who are moving horizontally to a similar job.

Obviously, the first-time employee will have much more to learn than the veteran employee who has moved to a similar position in another organization. But during those first days on the job, even the veteran employee is an F-2 employee because regardless of experience, the seasoned veteran needs to learn some of the basic rules, regulations, forms, and procedures of the new organization. Even such ordinary matters as where to sit and how to obtain supplies will have to be learned.

What normally differentiates newly hired F-2 employees is how long it takes them to learn the required skills. For some, the time span is fairly short. For others, it is long and tedious. Some of the reasons for this will be explained later in this chapter.

Newly hired employees are not the only F-2 employees. There are two other categories.

2. The F-1 employee who becomes motivated. Chapter 6 outlined the various ways that employees become F-1 employees. While lamenting over the fact that they had become F-1 employees, you also acknowledged that the goal was to help them regain their ability and motivation and to ultimately become F-4 employees. The first step in this process very often occurs when F-1 employees become more interested, enthusiastic, and motivated to do the job and evolve to an F-2 function level.

I am not suggesting that F-1 employees first become motivated and then learn the skills to do the job. This growth is not sequential. Employees do not do one thing first and then the next. What normally happens is that employees slowly gain in both ability and motivation, but one component is nearly always more dominant. My experience has been that employees more often exhibit stronger motivational tendencies as they grow and mature on the job. These employees represent one distinct way that an employee becomes an F-2 employee.

3. The employee who is moved either by choice or chance to a new position. These employees are working in an organization and either choose to move to a new position in which they lack the necessary skills or are forced into the position. How do employees find themselves in positions they did not want, were not trained for, or both? Most of you know the answer—perhaps even from personal experience. It may have been because the organization is downsizing and employees are shifted around. It may be because departments are combined and the only positions remaining are those in which employees have never been given any formal training. Or it could be in an organization—union or nonunion—where positions are eliminated, resulting in the "bumping" of one employee by another employee with seniority, who thus retains a job at a certain salary level or certain grade. Whatever the reason, employees find themselves in a new position, one that they are committed to mastering but also one for which they must learn new skills.

An employee may have become an F-2 employee for reasons other than these. What can be agreed upon, however, is that the F-2 employee has an interest in the job, wants to learn the skills or knowledge needed to succeed, and is motivated to do what is necessary to succeed on the job. From a supervisory perspective, what more could you ask for?

THE F-2 EMPLOYEE: A CASE STUDY

Before outlining how to apply the Functional Management Model to the F-2 employee, it is helpful to review a case study of a classic F-2 employee. This enables you to better appreciate the two dimensions—ability and motivation—used in assessing this type of employee. It also provides the foundation for better understanding the supervisory needs of the F-2 employee and how you can best supervise, motivate, and support this type of employee.

Jake was really pleased. He had just completed a long and arduous hiring process and had hired Karen as benefits specialist for his hand tools manufacturing company. Over 100 applicants, some with excellent resumés, had applied for the job.

Jake had narrowed the original list of applicants down to 12. Over an eight-day period, he interviewed all 12 applicants. Three clearly stood out. While each brought different types of experience to the position, all had received formal training and all had more than five years' experience in related areas. Jake decided to check their references and have the three top candidates back for a second round of interviews.

It was during the second round of interviewing that Karen really began to shine. She answered all questions with an air of confidence. She was personable and clearly knowledgeable. While the other two candidates also did well, Karen, in Jake's mind, stood out. She was clearly someone who could learn the necessary skills and adapt her previous knowledge and experience to this job. Jake felt both positive and optimistic about Karen's potential. When Karen's references checked out, he offered her the job.

Karen was thrilled and immediately accepted Jake's offer. While she was at first anxious about the application and interview process, she found that Jake's easy manner made her feel comfortable. What she learned during the interview process increased her interest in the job. She began to make calls to find out more about the company. The more she learned, the more hopeful she was that she would get the job. It was no wonder that she was excited about Jake's offer.

Let's summarize the events in the case study. Jake hired Karen because he believed that she had the background and potential to do the job. He recognized that Karen lacked some skills and would need to be trained, but she clearly demonstrated an eagerness and willingness to learn.

Karen was thrilled to get the job. She had relevant experience and was interested in the field of benefits management. While she also recognized that she would need to learn more skills, she saw the new job as a wonderful opportunity and was committed to learning everything she needed to know in order to succeed.

In many ways, this is the perfect F-2 work marriage—an employee who is willing, eager, and motivated to learn, and an employer who recognizes the new employee's needs and is willing to provide the necessary training. The challenge to Jake is to determine the appropriate training and to provide support and supervision. That's where the five-step Functional Management Model comes in.

APPLYING THE FUNCTIONAL MANAGEMENT MODEL TO F-2 EMPLOYEES

One of the most consistent pieces of feedback received from people trained in the Functional Management Model is that the model is logical. Supervisors not only understand each step, they understand why each step is important. They also understand the sequential relationship that ultimately leads to an employee-specific supervisory effort. Jake's efforts with Karen will help him to underscore this point.

As with F-1 employees, the five steps in the Functional Management Model apply to F-2 employees.

Step 1. Assess the Functional Level of the Employees

One point cannot be emphasized enough: you cannot successfully supervise an employee unless you clearly understand his or her functional level. Many supervisors report that the process of assessing F-2 employees is often easier than that of other employees. For one thing, many are newly hired and will have to learn some of the basic skills and procedures to do the job. For another, these employees are committed to learning what it takes to succeed. Often, if they know what skills they lack, they will tell you. They also will ask you how you will help them learn these skills.

In some cases, particularly for employees starting a new job, it may not be immediately apparent to them what they lack. Only after becoming involved with the job do these deficiencies become apparent. But once again, motivation makes F-2 employees normally very receptive to feedback and to the identification of skills or knowledge that they need to learn. Whether it seems obvious or not, you still must do a thorough assessment of these employees and determine their ability level. Do they have the necessary skills to succeed on the job? What skills or knowledge do they have and what do they lack?

An effective assessment of the ability level of an employee presupposes that you have a clear understanding of the concrete skills and expectations of knowledge that an employee must meet to succeed on the job. This goes beyond what is written in the job description for a particular position. For new employees like Karen, you must do three things:

1. Rely on what you learned during the interview process.
2. Hold an extended supervisory session with them to review the expectations and to determine what they know and don't know.
3. Assume that they need support in ability until you can personally document that they can do the job.

The reason for the third effort is simple. As a supervisor, you are responsible for ensuring that your subordinates get the job done in a qualitative and timely fashion. You need to be assured that new employees can do the job, and you can best do this by supporting and monitoring their efforts. You can begin backing off when you have enough clues to know that they can do the job.

Like ability, the motivational level of employees can be best assessed during the interview and initial supervisory meetings. Among the clues you look for are their eagerness to learn, their openness to new ideas, and their own self-initiative and follow-up.

It was very easy for Jake to assess Karen's function level. From the interview process, he knew that Karen had a solid foundation in benefit law and employee relations. He realized that she didn't know the organization's three specific benefit plans and would need to learn the various components of each. In his initial supervisory meetings, Karen also revealed her lack of knowledge of a number of technical and legal issues related to the industry that she needed to learn. Finally, Jake recognized that there were many organizational norms, rules, cultures, and so forth, that she would need to learn in order to get things done.

Karen's motivation level was obvious. She was anxious to learn. She had many questions and was constantly going out of her way to learn and succeed on the job.

Step 2. Define Employees' Needs and Your Supervisory Goals

Once you know the functional level of a specific employee, you are ready to develop your supervisory goals. These supervisory goals respond to the functional level of the employee.

The supervisor's primary goal with F-2 employees is to help them gain the skills and knowledge needed to succeed on the job. You defined any deficiencies in step one, so you know what training and skill development are needed.

In the initial stage of employees' new jobs, the supervisor may need to continually reassess their skills and knowledge in relation to the job. Often, only after employees have been tested on the job can you get a full picture of what their ability needs are. You can then adjust your training and skill development efforts to respond to these needs.

At the same time, you know that a major part of the training and education process is in the type of support you provide employees. Feedback, encouragement, and work-specific support are essential to helping F-2 employees maintain their confidence and motivation while they learn the necessary skills to do the job.

Finally, keep in mind that F-2 employees are potential superstars. While it is still not clear that they will succeed on the job, their motivation and interest in the job make them employees with great potential. Therefore, as an employer, you should be interested, at first on a limited basis, in setting the stage for their growth and long-term commitment to the organization. Begin exploring ways to help them learn and grow on the job.

Jake knew what he wanted to do. Karen was bright and motivated. Jake was well aware of Karen's positive attitude and her interest in the job. He saw that Karen might have a long-term future with the company.

Jake's goals were clear. He had to provide Karen with the training she needed to succeed. He would support and encourage her throughout the process and, on appropriate occasions—if it did not interefere with the primary goal of training her to do the job—provide opportunities that demonstrated the company's long-term commitment to her personal and professional growth.

For Jake or any supervisor to be effective, it is necessary to go beyond knowing what the employee's functional level is and know what the supervisory goals will be. The supervisor is then in a position to share these thoughts with the employee and to develop the specific supervisory strategies needed to achieve the goals.

Step 3. Clarify Your Assessment with F-2 Employees

What you are ultimately trying to do is to help your employees understand how they are perceived and how you plan to support them. In the ideal situation, you'd like to reach a consensus with your employees on both your assessment and strategies.

Why is this important? Because if you and your employees agree on what they need to learn and how you will supervise and support them, you will have created an optimal communication linkage. Employees will feel supported and will know what to expect. Best of all, with you both in agreement on your ultimate goals, employees will feel safer requesting additional support and training. Having a shared understanding makes it easier for you to provide the types of support the employee needs. An F-2 employee who agrees with your assessment is not only receptive to your support, he or she truly wants it. You could not hope for a better supervisory situation.

Even in the best of all worlds, however, you and the people you supervise may not be in agreement. You may feel that they are functioning at one level while they consider themselves at a different level, usually one that is higher. Or you may believe that employees need more training, but the employees feel that they already have had enough.

Your supervisory goal is to work this out with each employee and ultimately come to a consensus on your assessment, goals, and rationale. If it can't be worked out, the bottom line is that it's your call. You are the supervisor.

It has been the experience of most managers that this type of experience rarely happens with F-2 employees because they are highly receptive to identifying areas in which they need to learn new knowledge and skills. However, in the event that you are forced to take a position that is inconsistent with your employee's, you might want to seek an agreement concerning a time when you would review your assessment and what criteria you would set for this review.

It took Jake and Karen little time to reach a consensus. She agreed with Jake's assessment that she was an F-2 employee. The initial discussion on how to best train Karen was quickly resolved. In fact, during the process, Karen was able to request and receive additional training that she thought might be helpful.

Reaching a consensus with F-2 employees is usually fairly easy. Because they are motivated to succeed, they are also motivated to learn everything they need to do the job in a qualitative and timely manner. They also tend to be extremely appreciative whenever the organization goes out of its way to provide opportunities that enhance their personal or professional growth.

Step 4. Develop and Initiate Specific Supervisory Approach

Now you are ready to provide the F-2 employee with the most appropriate supervisory approach. Because F-2 employees are low ability/high motivation, their greatest need is for training and support. To a considerably lesser extent, you need to be alert to increasing their long-term commitment to the organization in comfortable ways.

Based on the Functional Management Model, F-2 employees need an S-2 supervisory approach: high direction, high work-specific support, and limited personal and professional development support. High direction ensures that you provide them with the training they need to do the job. High work-specific support ensures that they maintain high motivation while gaining confidence to learn the necessary skills. Finally, personal and professional development support helps the employees to realize that the organization cares about its workers. Organizations committed to their employees have employees that are committed to the organization.

Bear in mind that personal and professional development support doesn't need to be extensive for F-2 employees. One aspect of this support is providing employees with new opportunities to learn and grow professionally. Because F-2 employees are in the process of learning new skills, they are simultaneously receiving new opportunities to learn and professionally grow. The supervisor is actually able to provide two things at once.

While the S-2 approach for F-2 employees is consistent in all industries, the training that you provide changes. Obviously, training must be job-specific. The supervisor must know what skills and knowledge are needed to succeed in a specific job and then make it available. To a lesser extent, the same is true for work-specific support and for personal and professional development support.

In their meeting, Jake and Karen agreed that she needed training on the complex legal requirements related to the company's policies on disability and health insurance. She also needed training on how the agency handles unemployment claims. Because Jake's firm used a team approach to decision making, Karen would be expected, by virtue of her position, to lead at least one team on personnel-related issues. She would therefore need to learn the basic skills of team develpment and outcome-oriented planning.

Jake and Karen developed a training plan. They identified how Jake would monitor Karen's development and what Karen needed to do if she ran into difficulty. Regularly scheduled supervisory sessions were planned to review Karen's progress.

Finally, to reinforce the company's commitment to Karen's development, Jake agreed that the company would pay her $100 membership dues to the Benefits Managers Association, a professional association of benefits managers in the state.

Jake clearly responded to Karen's major supervisory needs. She needed training in specific areas. He provided it. She needed support and encouragement. Jake not only set aside time, he encouraged Karen to come to him for help with any difficulties. Finally, Jake began helping Karen understand the company's commitment to her personal and professional growth by paying for her membership in a professional association. In short, Jake was providing an ideal form of S-2 supervision to a classic F-2 employee.

Step 5. Monitor, Document, and Refine Your Supervisory Efforts

All supervisors hope that their supervisory efforts will have an impact on F-2 employees. Thanks to the supervisor, ideally F-2 employees learn all the skills needed to succeed and slowly evolve to an F-4 function level. This often happens but the reality is that F-2 employees could move in a different direction.

What happens if employees don't learn the basic skills needed to succeed on the job? No matter what you do, they are unable to pick up the knowledge or skills. Eventually they become frustrated about their inability to learn and slowly lose enthusiasm, confidence, and motivation. Now you are obviously supervising employees who have regressed from an F-2 to an F-1 level. This is not good news for the employees or you.

Supervisors must not only be aware of the things that cause employees to change functional levels but also recognize when employees have moved to a different level. If employees evolve to an F-4 level or slide to an F-1 level, you need to know it. Even if they remain at the same level, you need to know it. The reason is simple. If employees change functional levels, their supervisory needs change. An F-2 employee's needs are much different than those of an F-4 or F-1 employee. You will only know that your supervisory goals and behaviors must change if you continually monitor, document, and refine your efforts.

When you become aware of the evolution or regression of employees into a new functional level, you can streamline and focus your supervisory support on responding to their new needs. For example, if employees slide to an F-1 level, it doesn't make sense to strengthen your efforts to train and support their skill development. You should be supervising them much more tightly, particularly in view of the fact that they have lost much of their enthusiasm and motivation.

On the other hand, it is logical that if other employees learn the needed skills and evolve to an F-4 function level, you should reduce your emphasis on training and skill development and focus on responding to their personal and professional needs. If you fail to recognize that employees have evolved to an F-4 level, you are running the risk of insulting or demoralizing them by not acknowledging their growth.

And it is just as important to recognize when employees remain functioning at an F-2 level. If you know that they still lack the skills but remain motivated, you can continue to focus on skill development while still maintaining on a limited basis your interest in their personal and professional growth.

The only way to be aware of how employees are evolving is to continually monitor their progress. You do this in many ways: through your regularly scheduled supervisory sessions, specially scheduled review sessions, observation of performance, specific measurable goals collected in monitoring reports, and a range of other efforts designed to accurately monitor and measure employee progress.

Jake was determined to support Karen's growth. He recognized that the more she learned and the sooner she gained the skills necessary to succeed on the job, the quicker both Karen and the organization would benefit. This was clearly a win-win situation.

In order to monitor her progress, Jake did three things. First, he spent a great deal of time preparing an outline of Karen's major responsibilities and defining what constitutes success in her job; for example, the percentage of accurate disability claims filed, the time it took for people to get information on their benefits, and the development of certain products such as a new personnel manual.

Second, he defined the specific ways in which the organization would train Karen and ensure that she learned the appropriate skills. Jake and other members of the firm provided her with orientation and training on much of the work and culture of the organization. Jake arranged for Karen to attend an outside seminar on new developments in benefits law and also purchased training tapes on other technical issues. Because Karen was experienced and had some sense of some of the knowledge that she must acquire, Jake worked with her to identify other training needs. He approved of Karen's efforts to locate appropriate training.

Finally, Jake defined exactly how Karen's efforts would be monitored. Written reports would need to be submitted. Feedback would be obtained from staff. Review of reports in terms of timeliness and quality would take place. Weekly supervisory sessions would take place with him. There would be formal one-month, two-month, and three-month reviews. And there would be one day each month when Jake would work with Karen on a specific project to observe how she handled it. Finally, Jake agreed to let Karen know immediately how she was doing if he observed something worth noting.

Karen clearly exceeded Jake's expectations. She had no trouble adapting to the norms and culture of the organization. She learned quickly. She wasn't afraid to ask questions. If there was something that she didn't know about and needed training on, she immediately brought it to Jake's attention and provided him with a concrete recommendation on the means she would use to obtain the skills.

Jake, to his credit, provided Karen with ongoing feedback, support, and encouragement. He constantly praised her efforts and let her know that the organization deeply appreciated her work. He clearly followed the 80/20 Rule. Most of the time, certainly more than 80 percent of the time, he provided positive feedback. When he needed to provide constructive criticism and suggestions, his positive orientation made it easy for Karen to hear and learn from what Jake had to offer.

The result? In four months, Karen had learned all of the necessary skills to succeed on the job. She was looking for new ways to improve the benefits program of the organization and was proving to be a positive force in the company. Karen had clearly evolved from an F-2 to an F-4 function level. Thanks to Jake's positive supervisory support and Karen's commitment and motivation, Karen, Jake, and the organization as a whole were benefiting from the work of an F-4 employee.

GOOD NEWS/BAD NEWS FOR SUPERVISORS

Supervising F-2 employees can be exciting, challenging, and usually very rewarding. With newly hired F-2 employees, supervision can also lead to an interesting good news/bad news scenario.

When you hire new staff, you tend to hire F-2-type employees. They are glad to have the job and are usually highly motivated.

The good news applies to your new employees who developed the skills and knowledge to succeed on the job. You provided them with the right training and opportunities, and they soon were able to work independently. Thanks to you, they evolved to the F-4 function level—high ability/high motivation. You deserve credit and praise for your success.

But now the bad news. Let's assume the opposite happens. The employees failed to learn the new skills. They slowly became discouraged and lost their original enthusiasm and motivation. Now you have F-1 employees.

If the supervisor is entitled to take credit for helping employees learn and evolve to an F-4 level of functioning, shouldn't they also take the blame for employees who fail and slip to an F-1 level?

One of the comebacks that I often hear from supervisors is, "No, that's not necessarily so." They argue that the fault lies not in their supervision but in the fact that the employees had no capacity to learn the skills. They add, "She was hired for the wrong job."

"He just wasn't bright enough." "She wasn't truly committed." "He was the wrong person for the job."

Where then did the problem really originate? In most cases, supervisors hire or approve the employees who ultimately get the job. If you participated in the hiring process, aren't you responsible for employees who don't succeed? Maybe you didn't blow it in supervising the employees, but you blew it in hiring them in the first place. Either way, you've got to take some of the blame. If you accept the reality of the good news, you have to accept the bad news. Nobody said supervision was easy.

Of course, those of you who don't hire your own employees may feel you are off the hook. Maybe so. However, all that really means is that you have one thing the hiring supervisor doesn't have: a plausible excuse. Excuse or no excuse, you still have F-1 employees to deal with.

F-2: AN EMPLOYEE WITH POTENTIAL

There is no question that F-2 employees have incredible potential. They can be your organization's future leaders. They offer you the greatest potential for shaping. In many ways, their futures depend on you.

At some point in your career, you were an F-2 employee. You may have been motivated, but you lacked many of the skills needed to succeed. But you learned those skills and evolved to an F-4 function level, at which you are functioning today.

How did you arrive at this level? One reason certainly is that you were self-driven. Another reason, possibly the most important, is that you had a supervisor who recognized your needs and potential, and provided you with training, support, and encouragement. You looked to the supervisor for support and the supervisor came through. Today your F-2 employees are looking to you to come through for them. The question is, will you?

Chapter Eight

The Reluctant Performer
The F-3 Employee: High Ability/Low Motivation

I t can be a supervisor's worst nightmare: employees who clearly have the knowledge, skills, and ability to do the job. They've done it before and proved it to you. You know they can do it. They know they can do it. Colleagues and coworkers know they can do it. But something is wrong. They simply are not performing up to capacity. These employees seem to be sliding by, doing enough to avoid getting fired but little else. They appear uninspired and unmotivated, and don't seem to care. And it shows.

You're dealing with classic F-3 employees—those with the skills, knowledge, and ability to do the job, but who lack drive and self-motivation. The problems associated with F-3 employees aren't limited to the employees themselves. In today's workforce, which focuses on the team, no type of employee can have a more detrimental effect on the team than the F-3 employee. The reasons are simple.

When an employee has the knowledge, skills, and ability to do the job, you know it and so do most coworkers and colleagues. So when this employee is just sliding by, everyone else on your team is usually aware of it too. When coworkers see that an employee isn't performing up to capacity, they also begin to feel that the poor performance is affecting the team.

In today's highly competitive environment, organizations composed of people who are doing the minimal amount of acceptable work are destined to lose their competitive edge. And if organizations lose that edge, it won't be long before they are taken over, replaced, or closed.

Employees realize that low or marginal performance can undermine the viability of a team; this motivates many employees to strive for excellence and high productivity. But when hardworking employees begin to feel that they are carrying not only their own workload but also that of a coworker, something happens.

At first they are patient. They expect the low-performance employee to begin to show improvement. At the very least you, as the supervisor, will provide motivation. If nothing happens, they begin to get frustrated. If this continues, they start getting angry. Eventually they begin questioning why they should continue to work hard when you are allowing another worker to slide by. Before you know it, you have more than one F-3 employee. As more employees lose their enthusiasm and motivation, the morale of your team continues to slip. Strong teams are not made up of F-3 employees.

A THREAT TO YOUR CREDIBILITY

F-3 employees are more than just minimal performers and a serious drag on the morale of your team. They are also a serious threat to your credibility. Consider the following chart:

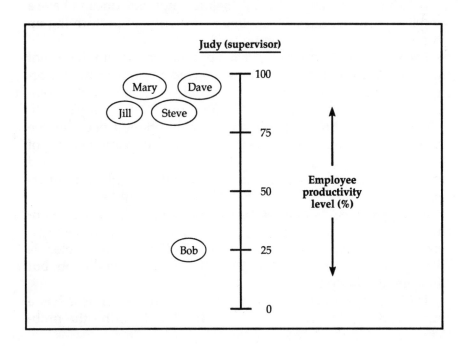

Judy is the supervisor of five employees—Jill, Steve, Mary, Dave, and Bob. The employee productivity level line represents how close to optimal performance an employee is functioning. You can see that Steve, Jill, Mary, and Dave are functioning well above 75%. While not all functioning at the same level, they are clearly performing at a high level.

Take a look at Bob. Bob is functioning well below 50% of capacity. He may be coming to work and doing an acceptable job, but the real problem lies in the amount of work he is doing. He is clearly not performing up to the organization's standards. Who's making up for Bob's minimal performance levels? Mary, Dave, Jill, and Steve.

These employees know that Bob is not carrying his share of the workload and they are not happy about it. They are frustrated with Bob, but they are even more unhappy and frustrated with another person, their supervisor, Judy.

Like employees in any workforce, the four employees are saying this about Judy: "Why doesn't she do something?" "Why is she letting Bob get away with this?" "Why doesn't she do her job?" "What is she getting paid for?"

Who has the problem? Bob? Absolutely not. Bob doesn't have a problem in the world. He's getting away with not performing up to expectations and he's getting paid for it.

The person with the problem is Judy. She has a team that is not functioning as a team. Morale is affected by Bob's low performance. Productivity is below what it could be if Bob was performing at the same level as other team members. Worse, Judy's credibility with her staff is being seriously questioned because she hasn't addressed a problem that has frustrated every member of the team. If she doesn't deal with Bob soon, she will be confronted with a serious crisis of confidence among the people she supervises.

F-3 employees, if not appropriately addressed, have the potential of seriously undermining the supervisor, team, and the organization as a whole. What makes them such a serious problem is that everyone knows that they have the ability to do the job, but they are not doing it.

This problem doesn't need to happen. The supervisor has a number of highly effective options available. Ignoring the problem, however, is not one of them.

HOW WORKERS BECOME F-3 EMPLOYEES

It is important to understand how employees reach the F-3 functional level. F-3 employees do not start out that way. As discussed in Chapter 7, new employees are nearly always F-2 employees. It is rare to find a new employee who is trained and skilled but undermotivated. New employees are usually highly motivated but lack certain basic skills. They are usually the opposite of F-3 employees.

On the Functional Level Chart, you can see that F-3 employees either regressed from an F-4 level or evolved from an F-1 level. From my experience in discussing F-3 employees in workshops throughout the country, there appear to be three major ways in which employees become F-3 employees.

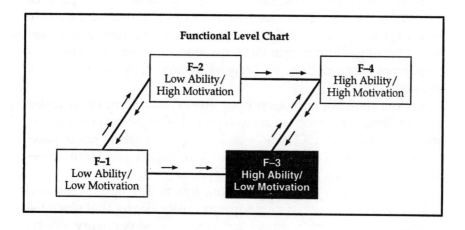

1. F-4 employees who lose interest and motivation in the job. F-4 employees who become less self-driven and less committed to doing the job are sure to become F-3 employees. They have proven that they have ability, but for whatever reason have lost their drive and motivation and are no longer producing at the level of which they are capable.

What makes employees like this *so dangerous* is their impact on your entire team. When other team members recognize these employees are not pulling their weight, they often become resentful because it puts more pressures on them. The team will look to you to do something about it.

How do employees who were formerly high performers suddenly lose some of their former motivation and productivity and become F-3 employees?

First, people do not *suddenly* become F-3 employees. They don't go to work one day as F-4 employees and the next day show up as F-3 employees. It is usually a slow, gradual process.

When one-time F-4 employees first came to the job, they had to learn the skills needed to succeed. Learning was a challenge and it was fun. As they learned, things became easier and their supervisors—assuming they were doing a good job—continually provided them with positive feedback, encouragement, and a great deal of work-specific support. It was only a matter of time before they became F-4 employees.

Even as F-4 employees, the learning and challenging aspects of the job did not stop. There were more things to learn. New ways to try things. Continued recognition for being a successful employee. New challenges and demands to respond to. It was a job that F-4 employees worked hard to succeed at, and they were, in fact, succeeding.

As time went on, without proper supervision, some of the luster and challenge of the job began to wear out. The job became routine and less challenging. There was little new to learn. Encouragement and positive feedback had far less impact and were sometimes construed as ridiculous.

Very often, however, supervisors ignore F-4 employees and provide minimal supervisory support, rationalizing that since F-4 employees are already proven performers, supervisory efforts should be focused on employees who have fewer skills and are less motivated and productive. This is a serious mistake, one that may haunt supervisors in the future.

F-4 employees who do not receive appropriate supervisory support and find the work becoming routine and—yes—boring discover that the enthusiasm and motivation of their early years beginning to ebb. Many F-4 employees become complacent and do only what they need to do to get by.

And as you will see shortly, these employees do not need extensive direction or work-specific support. On the contrary, supervisors who try to deal with the F-3 employees by increasing these supervisory behaviors will soon discover that they are not getting the results they had hoped for. Instead they may find that they are alienating the F-4 employee, furthering the lack of motivation.

2. F-1 employees who learn the skills yet remain unsure of themselves.   This way for employees to become F-3 employees is far less prevalent than the first example. There are, however, clear examples where this occurs.

For example, F-1 employees unable to learn the skills to do the job may originally have been highly motivated F-2 employees. Then they lost their motivation and are now struggling as F-1 employees. Many times a supervisor, out of sheer frustration or possibly through creative inspiration, comes up with a new way of providing training. Perhaps the supervisor discovers that these employees learn much better visually than auditorily and shifts the training approach to take advantage of this realization. Slowly, the struggling employees begin learning the skills needed to succeed. While motivation and skill development often occur together, one always dominates. In this case, skill development is the dominant characteristic and the employees evolve to an F-3 level.

Their motivation does not increase immediately—given that they had struggled initially on learning needed skills—because their confidence and self-initiation are low. Until they feel confident with new skills, they may be reluctant to initiate efforts without supervisory support and guidance. These employees evolve to an F-3 level and stay there only long enough to gain the supervisor's confidence and become more self-motivated. With the right supervision they ultimately can become F-4 employees.

3. F-4 employees who are forced into a less desirable position because of downsizing or other job changes.   During recent years, many industries have reduced their workforce and have redeployed staff. If you are the CEO of a company, you might call it "right sizing." If you are an employee not directly affected by the effort, you might call it "downsizing." But if you are an employee directly affected by the effort, you would call it devastating.

Downsizing is a horrible experience for many F-4 employees. If they are in a field where other people are laid off, you could argue that they shouldn't complain. After all, they still have jobs. But think how it must feel to F-4 employees. They became F-4 employees through hard work. They felt good about reaching a level of functioning where they were competent, recognized, and respected for what they had to offer. They were the captains of their destiny, which they had shaped and of which they were pleased and proud. And then downsizing.

Suddenly they are redeployed in positions that they don't want. All their work, all their efforts, and all their motivation cannot stop this. They have lost not only their jobs but also their sense of control over their future. As they settle into their new positions, they have to face the reality that they are no longer captains of their destiny.

Even though F-4 employees may have the skills needed to succeed in their new jobs, the discouragement and disappointment that comes from being displaced from a job that they want to one they are forced into—or encouraged to take for survival's sake—can cause some employees to lose their zest for the job. They may simply give up, doing just enough to get by. These employees have dropped to the F-3 function level.

ARE EMPLOYEES BURNED-OUT?

One question I often hear when describing F-3 employees is, "Are these workers simply burned-out?" First, it is important to understand clearly what is meant by the term *burnout*. Burnout originated as an engineering term referring to the complete burning up of missile or jet fuel. Burnout then moved into the vocabulary of management in reference to an attitude on the part of an employee that results in poor quality work or reduced productivity. Over the past 20 years, burnout has been discussed, dissected, and analyzed. It has been used to describe an array of functional problems of employees. Worse, it has been used to improperly label and stigmatize thousands of employees in all professions.

Many experts believe that the high achievers, the F-4 employees, are most susceptible to burnout. Burnout results from unrealistically high expectations on the part of these high achieving employees. Herbert J. Freudenberger, a New York psychologist and author of *Burnout: How to Beat the High Cost of Success*, describes burned-out employees as those who have "worn themselves out by excessively striving to reach some unrealistic expectation imposed by themselves or by the values of society."[1]

Burnout, however, is not the same as stress, another common problem among high achievers. Beverly Potter, a management consultant in Berkeley, California, sees burnout more as frustration on the part of the employees. Because they cannot meet their own expectations or those of others, they begin to feel helpless. As helplessness escalates, their motivation begins to slide. This helplessness can be real—for example, nurses doing their best to care for a terminally ill patient—or perceived, as in the case of employees who never receive any recognition or feedback from their managers despite superior performance. Burnout, unlike stress, more directly impacts an employee's motivation.[2]

Problems with Burnout

The problem with *burnout* is that it has such a negative connotation in the world of work that it can seriously hurt a person's reputation. If you question this, think about what your reaction would be if you were told that someone you were seriously considering hiring was burned-out. If you are like most managers, you would certainly be a little worried or reluctant to hire the person. You would at least have second thoughts.

In the trainings and in meetings with many organizations, supervisors were asked to answer the following question: "If you were told that a person applying for a job with you was a nice person but was also burned-out, what adjectives would you use to describe the person?" The adjectives consistently given by supervisors in all types of industries include

- Tired.
- Angry.
- Discouraged.
- Frustrated.
- Uninterested.
- Apathetic.

The common theme that is immediately apparent is that every term is negative. Every term suggests an employee who is overwhelmed and can't take it any more, who would be a risk to hire, and who leaves you with a negative impression.

Learnout vs. Burnout

Burnout says that from the employer's perspective, the employee can't take it anymore. The employee is in a powerless position. Burnout is a label that will be hard for the employee to overcome.

Is it possible that the employee is being mislabeled? Is it possible that the employee may not only be a good worker but be an exceptional worker? After all, most F-3 employees are former F-4 employees.

The trouble with burnout is that it places the problem squarely on the employee. But it is possible that the employee is not the problem. It is possible that the real problem is with the supervisor or the organization. It is possible that many of the employees regarded as burned-out are simply employees who have become bored and unchallenged on the job.

I believe that another term must be considered, a term that is far more appropriate for the vast majority of people who have been mislabeled burned-out. The new term is *learnout*. It refers to a very successful employee who has learned all there is to succeed on the job. After performing the job successfully for an extended period of time, the employee gradually becomes bored. There is nothing new to learn and the job is no longer challenging. Enthusiasm and motivation dwindle.

A New Perspective

With learnout the problem suddenly shifts from employees to the employer. No longer is it implied that employees can't take it anymore. Rather, the employees have taken everything that the organization has thrown at them, have succeeded, and are looking for more. The focus of the problem now becomes the organization, which is no longer capable of responding to or challenging the employee.

Learnout provides the supervisor with a new perspective, a new paradigm for looking at the employee. The employee is no longer viewed in strictly negative terms but as a person with the potential to succeed on the job.

No one is suggesting that burnout is an inaccurate term or that there is no such thing as burnout. Clearly some employees who have become overwhelmed, tired, or frustrated are burned out and have regressed to an F-3 function level. However, not all employees once thought to be burned out really are. Many are simply learned out. I don't know how many are really learned out and not burned out, but it is likely that more than half of the employees originally labeled burned out have been mislabeled and hurt by this term.

F-3 EMPLOYEES: A CASE STUDY

How can you deal with the one type of employee who is often regarded as the greatest challenge—or threat—to the supervisor? Let's follow through the five-step functional management supervisory process in a case study of an F-3 employee.

Mary was an accounting manager of a medium-size accounting firm located in a large metropolitan area. The firm had a staff of 60, of whom 40 were accountants. The rest were support staff. Mary had been in the firm for ten years and in her present position for three.

Mary supervised eight accountants, each of whom had been with the firm for a minimum of four years. The team member with the greatest longevity with the firm had been there more than 20 years. All eight accountants were highly trained and highly skilled. Mary's department had been recognized for consistently providing quality services. Things had been going well for Mary until now. One of the members of her team, Tony, has become a problem.

Tony has worked at the firm for seven years. He had graduated with honors from a prestigious university and had been eagerly sought after by many of the nation's largest accounting firms. He opted to go with Mary's firm because of its reputation and the opportunity it provided to get more quickly involved in all aspects of accounting. He learned fast, was the first to sign up for new projects, and over the last two years was emerging as one of the most respected members of the team. Now something seemed wrong.

For six months it had become increasingly apparent to Mary that Tony was a problem. He was slacking off. True, he has been meeting the minimal expectations of the firm, but just barely. His productivity has been gradually dropping although the quality of his work has remained excellent. Although he continued to be friendly, it appeared that Tony was less interested, enthusiastic, and motivated to do the type of job he was capable of doing.

This is a classic problem—an employee who was a high-functioning F-4 employee, but who is apparently losing his interest and motivation and has slipped into an F-3 function level. Fortunately, if you approach the F-3 employee appropriately, you can make some major gains within a short period of time.

APPLYING THE FUNCTIONAL MANAGEMENT MODEL TO F-3 EMPLOYEES

In many ways, F-3 employees are like other types of employees. They have specific supervisory needs and require supervisors who are aware of and respond to these needs. Once again, the five-step functional management supervisory process provides you with a clear, systematic means for supervising and supporting employees. The case study can be reviewed through the application of the five-step process.

Step 1. Assess the Functional Level of Employees

For F-3 employees, as with all employees, it is essential to assess their functional level accurately. You must know if they are motivated and have the ability to do the job. Only by finding that out can you be assured that you are supervising them appropriately.

You also must accurately document the facts that led to your determination about their levels of ability and motivation.

Documentation is probably most critical for F-3 employees because most of them are former F-4 employees who have lost their motivation. They may or may not be aware that this has happened. In either case, to effectively supervise F-3 employees, you must be prepared to share your honest perceptions with them. They need to know that you see them as undermotivated and functioning at the F-3 level. For employees who have difficulty recognizing or accepting this, accurate documentation of objective facts to support your contention are essential. When an employee says, "I am not short on motivation," you must be able to show the employee why you believe he or she is.

With Tony, Mary was able to trace his productivity levels. When it became increasingly apparent that something was wrong, she began to document other aspects of his performance. While Tony's quality remained good, he was producing less. Some of his reports were late. He was no longer participating in team meetings. Other team members were complaining that he wasn't carrying his share of the load. He was coming across as being uninterested and uninvolved. It was clear to Mary that Tony had slipped into an F-3 functional level.

Because motivation is often hard to document, it is critical that you obtain as many documentable examples as you can to support your position. Take your time. The more you are able to document, the easier it will be for you to do steps two and three.

Step 2. Define Employees' Needs and Your Supervisory Goals

If you have done a good job assessing the functional level of your F-3 employees, you probably already have a good idea of what their supervisory needs are and what your supervisory goals should be. The problem for F-3 employees is motivation, not ability. You do not need to focus on helping them to learn the job. They have proved to you and to themselves that they already know how to do the job.

F-3 employees need to be energized, to increase their motivation and enthusiasm. They need to make a stronger commitment to the organization and to their job.

Your goals are obvious: Work with F-3 employees so they become more motivated. Your accurate assessment should have identified many areas where they can improve their motivation. The challenge for you is to work with them on this improvement.

It was easy for Mary to identify Tony's supervisory needs and her supervisory goals. She knew that Tony's motivation had been slipping for some time. She knew in what areas it had slipped. She had clear documentation. And she knew what her supervisory goals must be to help Tony become more motivated. The challenge, as she saw it, was in determining how.

With employees who lack the ability to do the job—F-1 and F-2 employees—the supervisor can identify what skills the employees need and how to ensure that they receive the right training.

Motivation is a little different. F-3 employees need the supervisor's help in finding meaning to the job and reasons for motivation. However, what motivates one person may not motivate another. As a supervisor, you need to understand from the employees' point of view why they lack motivation. You also must work with them to identify what would help them to increase their motivation. Fortunately, step three provides that help.

Step 3. Clarify Your Assessment with F-3 Employees

Most supervisors dread telling F-3 employees—particularly former F-4 employees—that you are concerned because they seem to have lost much of their motivation. This is difficult to tell anyone. Dealing with the emotional response of employees may be more difficult, but you have to be honest with them. That is the only way that you can help them.

M. Scott Peck, an internationally recognized psychotherapist and psychiatrist, is a leading expert on personal and interpersonal growth and the need to honestly and openly confront problems. Peck's book on personal growth, *The Road Less Traveled*, has sold over three million copies. From his perspective, Peck explains why problems must be confronted: "Problems do not go away. They must be worked through or else they remain, forever a barrier to the growth and development of the spirit."[3]

Clarification means "talking with" rather than "talking at" your F-3 employees. You must use your meeting time to understand why they lack motivation and what can be done to restore it. Motivation is an individual thing, differing from employee to employee. What helps employees become more motivated also differs from employee to employee. Your challenge is to find out what caused the problem and how to fix it. The best way to do this is to ask the employees. After presenting your case for assessing them as F-3 employees, consider asking them three questions:

1. Are the facts and documentation that I presented accurate?
2. Why have you lost motivation? Or in the case of F-1 employees who became F-3 employees, why have you been unable to become motivated?
3. What can you and I do collectively to make the job more motivating and more responsive to your needs?

The key question is clearly the first. If you and your employees agree that the employee is functioning at an F-3 level, based on your facts and documentation, employees will usually be receptive to analyzing the causes and attempting to identify ways to help increase their motivation.

This is where doing your homework pays off. Most supervisors readily agree that solid documentation makes their job a lot easier. Supervisors trained in the Functional Management Model often share a little secret. When they assess an employee's functional level at F-3, supervisors increase their efforts to review and document examples of motivational problems. They do this knowing full well that the more documentation they have, the easier it will be for them to present their position to the employee.

What happens if you and your employees don't agree? No matter how thorough your documentation, they just won't buy it. They've got excuses. They say you're not being objective. They say you're wrong, that you just don't understand.

In fairness, you should give employees the opportunity to prove their case. Ask them to respond to your documentation. It is up to them to prove their point of view. But be firm. If they are unable to prove to you that *you* are wrong, you must take the responsibility for making the final determination. Remember one of the key realities of the Functional Management Model:

> If the supervisor and employee do not agree on the supervisor's assessment of an employee's functional level, the final decision is that of the supervisor.

Once your position has been established, you and the employee need to have an in-depth discussion to determine how this happened. Knowing the cause is obviously a big first step to devising strategies to resolve the problem.

Often employees are not sure what caused the problem. One strategy that many supervisors use is to allow employees time to think about it privately before talking about it again with the supervisor. Plan a second meeting to establish a consensus on their functional level. After this, a third meeting can be scheduled (usually within a week) to discuss the causes of the problem. During this discussion, the supervisor should strive to help employees further analyze the problems and to come up with as clear a perspective as possible. There may be one major reason or several. Perhaps employees felt they had been passed over for a job. Perhaps they had been at the job so long that boredom set in. Maybe changes on the team had a negative impact. Whatever the reason, it is critical that you make a strong effort to clearly understand the roots of the low motivation.

Once you have a sense of what is causing the problems, you are in a much stronger position to come up with ideas for addressing them. Whatever you decide to do, it is important that it be something that makes sense to employees. Your efforts will have limited effect if they don't make sense to employees or if employees aren't interested in or challenged by your strategies.

Be open and creative when working with employees to find ways to increase their interest and motivation. Encourage them to come up with suggestions to make the job more exciting and challenging. The more involved employees are with the process, the more committed they will be to seeing it succeed. Would employees be interested in training opportunities? Would being a mentor be of interest? What skills were they lacking in being passed over for a job? Could you help them get these skills? Would more frequent meetings with you help? Maybe the issue is the job itself. Could they apply for a transfer? Can you provide job sharing? If they are frustrated, why? Can you respond to this frustration? Would a change in shift help? Is there something you could do to help the team be more supportive? Are there quality-of-work issues you could initiate? Flextime? Support groups? Team-oriented projects? Are the employees' accomplishments recognized? Again, your challenge is to seek ways that respond creatively to your employees' needs. If you are successful, you will eventually help employees evolve to an F-4 function level.

Mary had done her homework. She had solid documentation and examples of work on which Tony had pulled back in his level of performance. Monthly status reports showed that he was doing 40 percent less work now than he was six months ago. He hadn't been on a committee in a year. Even Tony agreed that he had not participated in team meetings for a long time. With the exception of his work on the computer—Tony was a known computer enthusiast—his performance in nearly every other aspect of his job had declined.

At first Tony disagreed with Mary. He brought up work examples where he had obviously come through. But after listening to Mary and her identification of many examples of Tony's low performance, he had to agree. He had slowly become less enthused and motivated about the job. And while Mary never used the term "F-3," Tony had to agree that he was a person with high ability and weakened motivation.

During a follow-up meeting a week later, Mary discovered that Tony had been feeling neglected by the organization. When he had done work beyond what was expected, he received little recognition. He felt he had been passed over for project leader more times than he could count. What made him finally feel that the organization held him in low regard was that he was not asked to participate in the development of the organization's new MIS system even though he was recognized as the most knowledgeable staff person on computers.

Mary recognized two things. First, many of Tony's problems might have been avoided if she had been more aware of what Tony was going through. Second, what Tony wanted was reasonable. He was clearly someone who enjoyed challenges and appreciated having projects that he was responsible for.

They mapped out a series of trainings and joint projects that they could work on together. This way Mary could both support Tony's development and become better aware of his strengths and weaknesses.

When working with F-3 employees, you must continually strive to understand what their needs are and work with them to identify ways to respond to these needs. Remember, motivation is an individual issue that calls for an individual response. The more you know about your employees, the more you will be able to develop strategies that respond to their needs and help them increase their enthusiasm and motivation. The challenge is to implement the strategies in an effective manner.

Step 4. Develop and Initiate Specific Supervisory Approach

Once you have assessed the employees' functional levels, identified their needs and your supervisory goals, and come to a joint agreement on supporting their development, you are ready to implement your efforts.

Based on the Functional Management Model, F-3 employees need an S-3 supervisory approach: low direction, low work-specific support, and increased levels of personal and professional development support.

F-3 employees need to know that they are respected and valued, and that you are committed to working with them to respond to their needs and concerns. They don't need a lot of direction. Providing high direction to employees who have the proper skills can be a real turnoff, particularly your higher functioning employees. Therefore, F-3 employees require low direction and low work-specific support. Remember that "low" direction, does not mean "no" direction. In addition, F-3 employees, who usually function at minimal levels, need monitoring and limited amounts of work-specific support.

What F-3 employees really need is a high degree of personal and professional development support. This means following through with the employee what you discussed collectively in Step 3. Your ultimate goal is to provide employees with the opportunities to respond to their needs.

Mary was clear about what she needed to do. After discussing matters closely with Tony, they had mutually agreed that Tony would be given the opportunity to attend a number of trainings in which he was very interested. They had already agreed upon two projects over the next year. They would jointly chair the first one and Tony would be the sole chair of the second. Finally,

Mary had recognized that she needed to pay more attention to Tony's work and accomplishments, as well as those of other members of the staff. This actually became the first step in her quest to improve Tony's motivation.

The key is to follow through. Step three defines what you are going to do. Step four calls for you to follow through with that commitment. And if you succeed in following through with your commitment, you then monitor and refine your ongoing efforts.

Step 5. Monitor, Document, and Refine Your Supervisory Efforts

This may seem like a rudimentary step, but it is critical to supervisory excellence, particularly with F-3 employees.

You know that one premise of the Functional Management Model is that the best supervisory approach is one that responds to the Functional Level of the employee. Employees are not static; they can grow and change within an existing job. The only way you know they are changing is by a continual monitoring and documenting of these changes. In dealing with F-3 employees who are striving to increase their motivation and commitment, you must be aware of positive changes and support and reinforce them. At the same time be aware of how responsive employees are to your supervisory interventions.

By monitoring and documenting any changes in the employees' development, you can refine your supervisory approaches. As the employees continue to grow and evolve, you can share your observations and documentations with them. You let them know that you are pleased with any changes. As employees evolve to an F-4 function level, you can adopt the S-4 supervisory approach.

Although the initial meeting with Mary was uncomfortable, Tony had to admit that Mary was right. He was clearly losing his interest, enthusiasm, and motivation on the job. Not only was he frustrated, but also he had to admit that the job was less challenging.

Mary's session with him and the strategies that they agreed upon had worked wonders. Tony felt that Mary was clearly committed to helping him. She seemed more supportive of his efforts. She followed through with her commitments. And the two projects they had agreed to work on were not only challenging but exciting. Tony loved the challenges and was clearly motivated to succeed.

Mary learned two things. First, by spending a little extra time months ago, she might have been more aware of Tony's changing needs and have been more responsive. Second, it was clear that Tony had incredible potential. With the right—and consistent—supervisory approach, Mary could really help Tony excel.

Situations like Tony and Mary's are not unique. Every organization in the country struggles with F-3 employees. The vast majority of supervisors and managers in the workshops report that F-3 employees are the most challenging. But the case study shows that supervisors can have a dramatic effect on F-3 employees by being aware of their needs and providing supervisory support that responds to those needs.

The more aware you are and the more responsive your efforts, the more effective you will be in working with them.

Chapter Nine

The Model Employee
The F-4 Employee: High Ability/High Motivation

M ost CEOs know something that I'd like to share with you. F-4 employees make or break organizations. You are in good shape if you trained and developed enough of them and they hold most of the key positions throughout the organization. If not, you have problems, possibly big problems.

F-4 employees are the glue that holds the organization together. They are the employees you can rely on because they always come through. They are committed to the organization, to doing a high-quality job, to meeting goals, to supporting the efforts of their colleagues, and to ensuring the success of the organization. It is no wonder that F-4 employees are so critical to the success of the organization.

EMPLOYEES WHO IMPACT
THE ORGANIZATION

F-4 employees are critical to the success of an organization because they possess the key traits which ensure that the organization has the capacity and ability to produce high-quality products and to meet and exceed the needs and expectations of the people they serve.

The importance of F-4 employees is not limited to any one type of industry. They are the one group of employees who serve as the primary foundation for the success of any organization.

The F-4 employees are the employees who are proven reliable performers. They have high ability. They've studied, learned, and practiced. But F-4 employees have something else of equal importance. They are motivated, with the initiative and the drive to want to do a good job in a timely manner. These are employees who have the skills and the motivation to do the job properly.

Their value extends far beyond the work they do because their presence and behavior help establish the norms and culture of the organization. Other employees look up to F-4 employees. You may talk a good game, but it's your F-4 employees who play a good game and they play to win.

When you look at organizations that excel, it quickly becomes apparent that they have a sizable number of F-4 employees. It is equally apparent that their impact on the organization exceeds the actual work that they do. Organizations receive a number of added benefits from F-4 employees.

F-4 employees have a strong impact on team spirit. They are aware of other team members and recognize that the success of each member of the team affects the success of the entire team. F-4 employees volunteer to work on projects, tend to support other members of the team, and do what they can to support overall team efforts.

F-4 employees directly impact team performance and productivity levels. This is no surprise. An employee who is an exceptional performer or consistently meets or exceeds the standards for the team will certainly ensure or increase productivity levels. Other employees strive to follow the lead and standards set by F-4 employees.

F-4 employees serve as models or mentors for other employees, particularly F-2 employees. Employees know who the top performers are. Up-and-coming F-2 employees often try to emulate F-4 employees. Whether accomplished through a formal mentoring program or simply by observation, F-4 employees are role models for employees who are functioning at lower levels.

F-4 employees help ensure high-quality products and services. F-4 employees recognize that the success of their performance and that of the team and organization is dependent on a commitment to total quality. They strive for excellence and tend to demonstrate a personal commitment to high quality. They normally cannot accept inferior or inconsistent work because it runs contrary to this commitment.

F-4 employees affect the tone, norms, and culture of the team. F-4 employees answer the phone if no one else does. They help out when there is a backup at the copy machine. They volunteer for projects. They pick up paper from the floor. They are readily available to talk or do what they can to make the organization more positive and supportive. In short, they have a great deal of influence on the culture and norms of the organization.

The goal of supervisors is to help all employees become F-4 employees. The more successful you are at doing this, the more employees you will have who are independent, productive, and high functioning.

It is important to recognize that your F-4 employees will provide you with a unique set of supervisory challenges. Your worries are not over once they have achieved an F-4 level of functioning. Before identifying and addressing these significant supervisory challenges, you should review the primary ways that employees becomes F-4 employees.

HOW WORKERS BECOME F-4 EMPLOYEES

No one is born or starts off as an F-4 employee. F-4 employees have struggled to reach their ultimate potential. All have had to commit themselves to learning as much knowledge as possible in their field of experience. They've had to overcome disappointments and frustrations while staying focused and motivated. F-4 employees have often had the good fortune of having one or more supervisors who really cared, were highly supportive, and were effective role models.

Superstars who may have excelled at the same job in another department or another organization do not come into a new job as F-4 employees. Even superstars have to acclimate themselves to the new norms, rules, and cultures of their new job. And new employees who may have been F-4 employees in similar positions often need a short period of time to reestablish themselves as F-4 employees.

There are really two primary ways that employees become F-4 employees. The Functional Level Chart shows how employees tend to evolve to an F-4 level from either F-2 or F-3 functional levels.

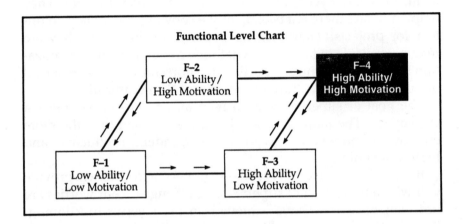

By understanding clearly how they make this evolution, you will gain some insight into how to supervise this type of employee effectively.

F-2 Employees Who Learn the Necessary Skills

Most new employees come into an organization as F-2 employees. They are highly motivated but need to learn skills essential to successfully fulfilling the expectations of the job. Once they have acquired the needed skills—assuming that they have not lost their original high motivation—they achieve an F-4 level of functioning—high ability and high motivation.

There is no set period of time that governs the evolution from an F-2 to an F-4 functional level, but in general, four factors affect how long it takes a person to evolve: difficulty of position, past experience, innate capacity to learn, and skill and support of the supervisor.

Difficulty of the position is probably the most obvious factor. Naturally jobs that require complex skills or knowledge will take more time to learn than those that are more simplistic. The more tasks or the more diverse the knowledge a person has to learn, the longer the learning curve normally will be.

The second factor that affects how quickly an employee will evolve to an F-4 level is the employee's past experience. The learning curve of an employee who worked in a similar position in another organization will naturally be shorter than that of someone just starting out. Another example is the employee who has worked in a similar or related field. The fiscal officer in a retail organization who moves to a health service organization might have an easier time than the employee who is just entering the fiscal world. Both will need to learn new skills, but the first-time employee will have to learn far more of the basic skills.

The employee's innate capacity to learn specific skills or knowledge is the third element determining the evolution from F-2 to F-4. This is a complex mix of the person's intelligence, learning style, attention span, and many other variables that determine how easily a person can learn something. To understand this variable, you need only look at yourself. Did you learn things at different rates? Were you faster or slower than your friends in learning to hit a baseball? How about math? Or how to type? Or ride a bike? Use a computer? Whatever the knowledge or skill, some people learn faster than others.

Finally, the fourth variable that affects the rate that an employee moves from an F-2 to an F-4 level is the skill and support of the supervisor. Not all the blame or responsibility lies with the employee. The skill and support of the supervisor may be the single most important variable. As a supervisor, you must be sensitive, patient, thorough, and responsive to the learning pace of your employees. Just as they learn at different rates, they also have different learning styles. Some learn more easily by observing, others by hearing instructions, and still others by slowly trying out what they learn. You will be a more effective supervisor if you are aware and responsive to each employee's learning style. The Supervisory Assessment Form provides a number of other questions that you should ask yourself to ensure you are providing optimal supervision.

This form is not exhaustive but simply a checklist of a few key questions supervisors should ask themselves as they try to provide optimal supervision to any employee.

Supervisory Assessment Form

Yes/No

_____   Am I meeting with the employee on a regularly scheduled basis?

_____   Have I identified all of the knowledge and skills that the employee needs to learn?

_____   Is the employee's learning rate negatively affected by missing tools or resources?

_____   Am I providing the employee with appropriate levels of feedback?

_____   Do I encourage the efforts of the employee?

_____   Have I asked the employee how I could provide better help?

_____   Am I consistent in my efforts with the employee?

_____   Am I readily available when the employee seeks help or has questions to ask?

_____   Am I a model of the type of behavior that I would like to see in this employee?

_____   Is there anything that the team (or other colleagues) can do to help this employee?

F-3 Employees Who Were F-4 Employees

Supervisors certainly deserve credit for supporting the efforts of F-3 employees to regain their motivation.

In Chapter 8, you saw how F-4 employees may lose their motivation and slide to an F-3 function level. Over a period of time, and with the proper balances of personal and professional development support, direction, and work-specific support, employees find new challenges and new meaning on the job. Their motivation slowly begins to increase. With renewed commitment on the part of employees and the consistent support of the supervisor, they return to an F-4 level of functioning.

F-1 Employees Who Gain Skills More Rapidly Than Motivation

F-1 employees lack both the ability and motivation to do the job. The supervisor must focus very heavily on helping them learn the necessary skills while also trying to encourage their learning. Because many F-1 employees have lost their confidence, they often learn the skills or knowledge before they are fully confident and self-driven and willing to do the job on their own. They come across as timid or unsure of themselves. These F-1 employees tend to evolve directly to an F-3 level. With the proper supervisory support and encouragement, they will slowly realize their strengths and potential, gain confidence, and ultimately acquire the motivation to evolve to an F-4 function level.

If you have never encountered these employees, you might be surprised to learn how difficult it is to help them gain the confidence and motivation to become F-4 employees, even though they clearly have the skills to do it. These employees may feel this way because of previous failures at work. Their behavior could reflect earlier life experiences that were detrimental to their confidence and motivation. Whatever the reasons, the supervisor must be prepared to help them regain their confidence and motivation and to realize their full potential.

While the employees may have become F-4 employees in different ways, the challenge to supervisors is to find creative ways to help F-4 employees maintain their enthusiasm, commitment, and motivation. This can be a real challenge to supervisors, particularly if they don't approach supervision in a realistic manner.

THE F-4 EMPLOYEE: A CASE STUDY

To better understand how to effectively respond to F-4 employees, it is helpful to follow the same format used in earlier chapters on F-1, F-2, and F-3 level employees. The application of the Functional Management Model to the case study shows how the systematic process adjusts to F-4 employees.

Remember that the Functional Management Model is a highly fluid and employee-specific supervisory management model.

While it calls for a systematic, five-step approach to supervision, the model is designed to ensure that supervisors adjust their approach in response to the supervisory needs of each employee. The employee-specific nature of the model is one of its most obvious strengths.

Home care is one of the fastest growing fields in the health care industry. It's the field where nurses, home health aides, therapists, and other health care professionals provide a range of medical services to people in their homes.

Sarah had been in the home care field for nearly 10 years. She had entered the profession immediately after graduation from nursing school. She loved her job, was promoted to supervisor, and three years ago was named director of one of the agency's area nursing teams.

At present she supervises eight nurses. While they are at different levels of functioning, one nurse, Colin, has consistently stood out. He has been a member of the team for two years. The technical quality of his work is excellent. He is incredibly reliable and is well liked by his patients. Colin has received more letters of recognition and appreciation from patients than any other nurse on Sarah's team.

Having recently learned the Functional Management Model, Sarah was in the process of assessing each of her nurses. She had already completed assessing six nurses and was now ready to begin applying the model to Colin.

APPLYING THE FUNCTIONAL MANAGEMENT MODEL TO F-4 EMPLOYEES

If there is only one term that should be used with F-4 employees, it is *partnership*. F-4 employees have earned your respect and the right to be partners in the process of defining how to best help them maintain their motivation and commitment. The best way to show them that you support and respect their capabilities, commitment, and performance is to use a partnership or collegial approach to supervision. The collegial approach means that F-4 employees can be active partners in defining what they need and how they will receive it. Do not worry that you will lose your authority or control. As the supervisor, you always reserve the right of final approval.

The implicit goal in supervising F-4 employees is to convey in the strongest way possible that they are valued. Employees who are valued return this feeling with a strong commitment to the people and organizations who care about them. It makes sense that supervisors should work to establish an environment that reinforces employee development.

With this assumption in mind, you can focus on supervising and supporting F-4 employees using the five supervisory steps in the Functional Management Model.

Step 1. Assess the Functional Level of Employees

Assessment plays a dual role in supervising F-4 employees. First, the assessment is essential to clearly documenting the functional level of the employee. It allows you to verify and substantiate their high ability and high motivation. The search for documentation is the same for all employees. You use all the tools at your disposal to conduct the assessment. You reflect on your own observations. You review reports. You review interactions you have had with the employee. You ask for feedback from other supervisors of the employee.

Second, the assessment process reassures you that the employees are truly F-4 employees. This makes it easier and more comfortable for you to encourage their active involvement in defining how their supervisory needs can best be met.

For Sarah, Colin was easy to assess. She had observed his work directly and knew he was an extremely competent nurse. He always attended training on new medical procedures and was often asked by other members of the team for advice. In many ways, he had become an unofficial mentor to the newer staff.

His competence was matched by his motivation and commitment. He was incredibly reliable and motivated. He was rarely out sick and Sarah couldn't remember the last time he was late. Colin clearly excelled on every measure that Sarah could think of.

In many ways, Colin's assessment proved to be the easiest for Sarah to make. Her direct observation and consistent reports

made it readily apparent to Sarah that Colin was an F-4 employee. While doing the assessment, collecting documentation,
and substantiating it, something else became apparent. Colin
was an extremely valuable member of the team. It was important that Sarah make the necessary efforts to help maintain his
high levels of performance.

Often supervisors are surprised at what they discover during
the assessment stage. It is not uncommon for supervisors of F-4
employees to reach a high level of recognition of the importance of
a specific employee. They may suddenly realize that they may
have been taking their top-performing F-4 employees for granted
and ignoring them. This can be a dangerous attitude to have.
Just as your favorite plant will surely shrivel up without water
and the attention it needs, your top performers will slowly lose
their luster if they don't receive the attention they need and deserve.

Step 2. Define Employees' Needs and Your Supervisory Goals

Defining the supervisory needs of F-4 employees differs significantly from that of other employee levels, particularly F-1 and F-2
employees. Supervisors are in a good position to know what
technical skills F-1 and F-2 employees lack and to recognize that
these skills must be met if the employee is going to succeed on
the job.

F-4 employees have already mastered the technical skills. The
supervisor's challenge is to find ways to help them maintain their
high level of performance. The best way to meet the needs of top
performers is to work with the employees. In essence, you are
identifying personal and professional development efforts that
respond to F-4 employees' needs while strengthening their commitment and contribution to the organization.

While the specific needs to which you respond may not be clear
at this stage, your goal with F-4 employees is clear. They need the
S-4 supervisory approach: low direction, low work-specific support, and extensive personal and professional development
support.

F-4 employees clearly know how to do the job, so you don't have to provide them with much direction. The direction you do provide is normally that of monitoring and coordinating their efforts, not in providing training. Providing employee-specific personal and professional development support is obviously more complex and more extensive.

It was clear to Sarah that Colin was an F-4 employee. While she had some idea of what Colin found interesting and exciting, she knew that she would need to work with him to clarify specific ways in which she could support Colin's continued high level of performance. She knew that the best vehicle was in finding ways to respond to his personal and professional development needs.

It was also clear to Sarah what her supervisory goals should be. She needed to continue to monitor and coordinate the efforts of Colin with the rest of the team. Her primary focus, however, would be to work with Colin to maintain his motivation and commitment to the organization by responding aggressively to his needs for personal and professional development support.

Step 3. Clarify Your Assessment with F-4 Employees

You must strive to reach a consensus with F-4 employees on your perception of their functional level. Unlike other employees at functional levels you will rarely get an argument from F-4 employees. Let's face it: Not many people would argue with a supervisor who says they are terrific, high-performing employees.

The real challenge is in working with F-4 employees to identify ways to keep the job as interesting and exciting over time as it is today. You do this by sharing with the employee your assessment of his or her functional level and the outline of your goal of keeping the job interesting and exciting.

F-4 employees have a fairly clear sense of the realities of the organization. They know what can and cannot be done. The challenge for you is to find out what can be done to respond to the employees' needs that also fits within the realities of your organization.

Colin was clearly pleased by Sarah's assessment of his performance. He loved his job and the people he was working with.

Even though he always felt that he was doing a good job, it was good to have that validated by his supervisor.

Following Sarah's review of her assessment of Colin, she began discussing her hope that his job should be one that Colin would continually find interesting and motivating. She offered to work on efforts that responded to his personal and professional development. As she explained to Colin, her intent was to work with him to identify opportunities that Colin would find helpful.

Nothing was resolved during the first meeting. In fact, it took two more meetings before Sarah and Colin were able to identify areas of interest. Colin was interested in taking a recently established course on new developments in high-tech therapy. He was also interested in playing a bigger role in supporting and training other members of the team and clinical staff in other sections of the agency.

These were clearly efforts that Sarah felt would benefit both Colin and the organization. She committed herself to exploring how to make these potential opportunities a reality.

By involving F-4 employees in the assessment process, you dramatically increase the likelihood that whatever is developed is truly responsive to opportunities that they value. You greatly reduce the trial and error. You reduce guesswork by going to the source of knowledge—the employee.

Step 4. Develop and Initiate Specific Supervisory Approach

What you come up with will differ from employee to employee. Many employees will seek more training. Others will seek involvement in decision making. Others might want to take responsibility for a particular project or effort. Remember, there are no canned answers. Each effort must be individually defined and worked out.

As you read this, it is important to note that the ultimate goal is always ensuring that the employees maintain or strengthen their exceptional performance level. The goal is not to have employees involved exclusively in personal and professional development efforts. These are simply vehicles that support the primary goal of maintaining a high level of employee performance. Obviously, the vast majority of work time should be spent on the employee's primary task. Personal and professional development support enhances that experience and strengthens their potential.

Note the amount of time it took Sarah and Colin to identify potential areas for personal and professional development. Because these efforts need to be employee-specific, it takes time to work with the employee to come up with realistic opportunities.

The opportunities do not have to be dramatic or extensive. For F-4 employees who are obviously enjoying their jobs, providing opportunities for personal or professional growth simply makes the job more satisfying. Interestingly, for those F-4 employees who might be losing some of their enthusiasm, these personal and professional development enhancers are often the critical variable that helps reenergize them and keep them at an F-4 function level.

Through the provisoin of personal and professional development support, you clearly convey to F-4 employees that the organization respects, appreciates, and cares about them. By providing forms of support that respond to their specific needs, you provide a concrete reason—an incentive—for the employees to maintain their exceptional performance. And by involving them in the process of defining those needs and desires, you empower the employees and strengthen their investment in something they helped to design.

What Sarah needed to do was to be clear. While she continued to monitor Colin's performance and coordinate his efforts using the normal supervisory systems, she also worked with Colin to respond to his needs for personal and professional growth.

They had determined in step three that Colin would appreciate having the chance to take a course on high-tech therapy and also to increase his mentoring of new staff—both efforts that would benefit the organization.

In meeting with Colin, Sarah agreed that the agency would pay for his course. She also agreed to work with Colin and two staff members from another department who were interested in starting a mentoring program. Together they would have the opportunity to develop a new internal program that would benefit everyone in the organization.

Colin was pleased that he would have the opportunity to obtain two things in which he was very interested. He was also pleased with the level of support and recognition he was receiving from Sarah and the organization as a whole. It made him value all the more his involvement with the organization.

Remember to be flexible and supportive whenever you implement a specific supervisory approach. Be sure that whatever you do responds to the very personal and individual needs of each employee.

Step 5. Monitor, Document, and Refine Your Supervisory Efforts

Most supervisors consider this common sense. If you truly want to gain the most from your employees, including F-4 employees, you must be continually aware of their progress.

No one stays the same forever. What may be of interest to employees today may be boring tomorrow. Are you still interested in the same things at work today as you were a year ago? Naturally some things continue to hold your interest, but you probably gained or lost interest in other things during the past year. The same is true of your employees.

How you monitor your employees depends on your organization and its supervisory procedures. Certainly you will use personal observations and what you learn in the supervisory sessions. You might also use your review of reports and customer feedback reports. The procedures used should give you an accurate picture of the progress and evolution of your employee.

You also should let your employees know how they will be monitored. This will help them to realize more fully that you are committed to supporting the efforts you mutually agreed upon. It also lets them know that your effort is not a one-shot deal but the beginning of an ongoing effort to support their growth and development.

Once Sarah and Colin had agreed on the ways Sarah would support his efforts, Sarah discussed with Colin how she would monitor them. In addition to their regularly scheduled supervisory meetings, she would accompany him on home visits at specified times. She would also be working with him on the mentoring program. Sarah further stated that she would continue to review the progress notes and Colin's monthly report.

For Sarah, the discussion about how she would monitor and refine her support was important. She wanted to convey to Colin that she was committed to supporting his efforts. She wanted to be constantly aware of what was required of her to help Colin continue to achieve at an optimal level.

Supervisors are wrong to believe that their work is over once a supervisory plan has been mutually agreed upon. The key to successful supervision is to realize that nothing is stagnant. You've heard the saying: "Change is inevitable." Successful supervisors know that change is a reality. The only way that they will be aware of changes—including those that occur when employees lose their enthusiasm and slip into an F-3 level—is by monitoring their ongoing performances.

These high ability/highly motivated employees are the backbone and foundation of exceptional organizations. This is a major reason why you cannot take the chance of ignoring or taking your F-4 employees for granted.

THE UNFORTUNATE REALITY

There is one reality that you will need to face. No matter what you do, what you say, or how responsive you are, you will lose some of your F-4 employees. They are going to leave you and go somewhere else to work.

Why do they have to leave, you ask? The answer lies in the realities of corporate life. Most corporations are like pyramids with more people at the bottom of the organizational structure than at the top. There are more workers than supervisors, more supervisors than senior managers, and as all senior managers know, only one CEO.

Employees know that the further up the career ladder they go, the more responsibility and authority they will be given. The aura of authority, power, and responsibility is a great draw for many of these employees. So too is the greater recognition and status that goes with higher positions.

If all that is not enough to entice F-4 employees to move from their present position to a higher or more responsible one, there is another reality—money!

One could debate whether it is right or fair for top managers to earn so much more than line employees, but the purpose here is to simply acknowledge the reality. People who are higher up in the organization tend to make more money than those in lower positions. For F-4 employees, particularly those with families or other responsibilities, a surefire way to reduce financial strain is to move into positions that pay more money. When you put it all together, it is obvious that F-4 employees have numerous incentives to leave their positions: There is nothing more to learn. They are no longer challenged. They feel that they are not truly appreciated. It is time to move on. They learn of a new position that pays more money and the difference is large enough for the change to be worthwhile. Greater learning opportunities, more challenges, more responsibilities, more power, greater recognition, and more money—those are powerful incentives.

How to Keep Your F-4 Employees

There are ways to keep your F-4 employees. They like challenges. They like to be successful. And they like to be appreciated. The more you can respond to their personal and professional development needs, the greater the potential that the job they hold now will continue to be rewarding. Your challenge is to work with your F-4 employees on personal and professional opportunities. You must come up with meaningful activities and experiences that are appropriate for them within the realities of the employees' position and your organization's environment.

But remember, supervisors can only influence their employees' commitment up to a point. When F-4 employees are ready and willing to leave, then you are going to lose them.

Three Realities of Losing an F-4 Employee

You should keep three factors in mind as you face the reality that you are going to lose one of your model employees. First, under your supervision this employee has come through for you. But you must also acknowledge the superior performance achieved while he or she was with you. That's why you rated the employee as an F-4.

Second, there are important reasons why the employee became an F-4 employee. The employee worked hard to succeed and deserves recognition and credit for this accomplishment. Not all employees reach an F-4 level of functioning.

Another reason the employee became an F-4 employee is because he or she was lucky enough to have had you as supervisor. You helped the employee to grow and gain the confidence to succeed by being directive when you had to be. The employee's success is a reflection of your success and you deserve recognition and credit for helping to develop this model employee.

The third factor is a reflection of what you did in your career. You, like most supervisors, were an F-4 employee in previous positions. You learned what you could and when you were ready, you made the choice to move on.

You might also realize that as a supervisor, you are an F-4 employee now. Isn't it conceivable that you will be making the same decision in the near or distance future that your F-4 employee is now making? It's all part of the reality of being an employee in our modern workforce.

Chapter Ten

Applying the Model to Your Most Challenging Employee

O ne of the most frustrating things about many of the books and articles on the supervision and management of staff is that they never really finish what they set out to do. They present a new theory or model. They discuss it. They may even present some concrete examples to help you understand it better. Then they stop.

They almost always encourage you to "try it, you'll like it." Like many managers searching for a better mousetrap, you probably were moved to "try it." But something isn't working. What do you do? You might reread a book to see if you missed something. What you discover, however, is that the author missed something—he or she failed to address a particular problem related to the theory.

People who attended any of the thousands of management trainings might also recognize this problem. You listen attentively to the trainer or presenter. You take notes. You participate in group exercises. If you felt the training was successful you might have left the training excited, confident, and ready to test your newly learned skills or knowledge. Unfortunately, you may soon discover the same problem as the reader. Something isn't going exactly as you expected. A problem develops. Employees don't respond the way they are supposed to. The things you learned may not seem as practical or as simple as they did when the trainer presented them.

You are left to flounder. You try to wing it and hope you can improvise and come up with the answers that you couldn't find or didn't learn. Sometimes, out of frustration or lack of confidence, you may abandon your new knowledge and fall back to doing things the same way you used to.

MAKING THE FUNCTIONAL MANAGEMENT MODEL WORK

This chapter and the next will respond to this reality. Rather than simply presenting the model, I want to help you test it. I want to give you the chance to apply the model to your most challenging employee.

The text is accompanied by forms and questions to assist you in learning how to use the Functional Management Model. You will work through the biggest problems that supervisors normally face when applying the model. If you can successfully apply the model to your most challenging employee, you should find it even easier to apply it to those employees who are less challenging.

The goal is to push you to think through what you are doing thoroughly. You must not only understand what you have to do but also why. The more you work with the Functional Management Model and have the opportunity to have your problems addressed and your questions answered, the more comfortable and confident you will be in using the model. Once you know the Functional Management Model and how to apply it, and are comfortable, confident, and motivated to use it, you will have achieved the status of a true F-4 level supervisor. Let's get started.

SUPERVISING YOUR MOST CHALLENGING EMPLOYEE

Why am I using the word *challenging* instead of words like *problematic* or *unproductive*? The answer is that your most challenging employee may not be problematic and may not be unproductive. As you learned in Chapter 9, an F-4 employee may be the most challenging employee for many supervisors.

You may be surprised to learn that what earns an employee this label has less to do with the employee and more to do with the knowledge, confidence, and feelings of the supervisor. The employee who is a challenge for one supervisor may be easily understood and supervised by another. The first supervisor may have lacked the experience or knowledge to deal effectively with the employee while the second supervisor may have had previous experiences with this type of employee and knows what to do. The personality of the employee may be one with which the first supervisor was comfortable while the second was not. Or it may be because one supervisor was more knowledgeable and skilled than the second.

Another reason—one that I see often—has to do with a supervisor's confidence in dealing with certain levels of employees. Supervisors who may be very comfortable dealing with F-2, F-3, or F-4 employees may be uncomfortable dealing with F-1 employees. They may feel at ease providing personal and professional development support to employees they know have the skills to succeed or to employees who may lack the skills but who are clearly motivated to learn. But when it comes to employees who have neither the ability nor motivation to do the job, supervisors may be intimidated, fearful, or unsure about supervising them. For this supervisor, the F-1 employee is clearly their most challenging employee.

The opposite could also happen. There are many supervisors who are very comfortable being directive. They can provide clear direction and training. They have no trouble confronting and setting clear limits on the F-1 employee. But they are far less confident in working in a more collegial way with high-functioning F-3 or F-4 employees. Most supervisors have at least one level of employee they personally find more challenging than other levels.

You focus on your most challenging employees because if you can successfully apply the Functional Management Model to them, you will certainly feel confident applying the model to employees you were previously comfortable supervising. If this model truly helps you become a more effective supervisor by improving your ability to deal with your most challenging employees, that will be a major step forward.

Identifying Your Most Challenging Employee

Before applying the five steps of the Functional Management Model, you must take one "pre-step." You must identify one employee that you want to supervise more effectively and look at honestly. This is a real test of the applicability of the model.

It will probably take you a fraction of a second to zero in on one or two employees who are your most challenging employees. Don't be surprised if you find yourself focusing on two employees at two different functional levels. One may be an F-1 employee. The other may be an F-3 employee. Given the range of personalities, attitudes, and interpersonal skills your employees possess, this often happens.

Determine which employee is at a functional level that you find particularly difficult to manage. You will undoubtedly have other employees at this level in the future so, considering you recognize your own difficulties supervising this level, that is the employee on whom you should focus. Next you need to understand why that employee is so challenging. The Employee Review Form will help you in this process.

When filling out the Employee Review Form, be as objective as possible. Because you are asked to focus on your most challenging employee, you might tend to play down your frustrations and not acknowledge just how challenging this employee really is.

In answering why you find this employee so challenging, be specific. If you sense that the employee shows you no respect, acknowledge that. If you feel that the employee can't follow directions or has difficulty learning new skills, say it. If the employee has a bad attitude, list it. The key is to be sure that you have a clear sense of why you feel that this particular employee is your most challenging employee.

At the same time, you also must be able to recognize that all employees—even F-1 employees—have strengths and weaknesses. If you are about to say, "My most challenging employee has no strengths," then you are either failing to assess the employee honestly or you've waited far too long to address and initiate termination procedures on that employee. My belief, however, is that all employees have strengths, and it takes a mature supervisor to recognize this even when he or she is frustrated.

Employee Review Form

1. Challenging employee's name   _____

2. How long has this employee worked for your organization?   __
   _____

3. How long have you supervised this person?   _____

4. What does this employee do that you find so challenging?   ____
   _____
   _____
   _____

5. What are the employee's greatest strengths?   _____
   _____
   _____
   _____

6. What are the employee's greatest weaknesses?   _____
   _____
   _____
   _____

7. What have you done as the employee's supervisor that has helped
   his/her performance?   _____
   _____
   _____
   _____

8. What have you done that has not helped?   _____
   _____
   _____
   _____

9. How do you feel about supervising this employee?   _____
   _____
   _____
   _____

In addition to identifying their strengths and weaknesses, a fair assessment must also include what has and has not worked when supervising your challenging employees. You've initiated supervisory actions that turn out be so brilliantly effective that their productivity and motivation go up. You feel like a supervisory superstar.

At the same time, you have probably initiated actions that have bombed. Instead of motivating employees your actions brought an opposite reaction. Instead of feeling like a superstar, you felt like a falling star. Cheer up! It happens to all supervisors. But you want to learn from your successes and your failures. At the very least, you don't want to make the same mistake twice.

Finally, how do you feel when supervising this employee? Do you find yourself tense and anxious? Do you feel angry or frustrated? Are you really fair and reasonable or are you always looking for something to criticize? Do you look forward to meeting with the employee or are you more interested in avoiding the meeting or ending it as soon as you can?

It is important when filling out the Employee Review Form that you acknowledge the feelings you have with this employee. Your feelings may be subtle. They may be overt. But whatever they are, they come out in your interaction with that employee. It is important that you are aware of your feelings in supervising and interacting with this employee because those feelings are probably expressed in your actions. And your actions will obviously be either a positive or negative catalyst for the employee's reaction. To acknowledge how you feel will increase the chances that you will be more sensitive to the unique needs of the employee.

APPLYING THE MODEL TO YOUR MOST CHALLENGING EMPLOYEES

As soon as you have a clear understanding of who are your most challenging employees, you are ready to implement the five-step Functional Management Model.

Step 1. Assess the Functional Level of Employees

If you were diligent about the way you defined your most challenging employee, you are probably half, if not all, the way toward determining the employee's functional level. Before you jump ahead, a word of caution. Many supervisors tend to skip over the assessment step or give it only a passing glance. They rationalize that they have worked with the employee and have a clear sense of his or her functional level. In most cases, the supervisor is right but in a few cases they may be wrong. So, don't take the chance.

The Functional Level Assessment Form requires you to take a thorough look at your employee. The two key questions concern the employee's ability level and motivational level. Notice that for both ability and motivation, you are asked to document why you rated the employee "high" or "low." It is important that your determination be based on fact, not feeling.

Functional Level Assessment Form

1. Employee's name   _____

2. In terms of the overall job, is this employee's ability level high or low?
   ABILITY LEVEL: _____

3. What are the reasons you rated the employee's ability level the way you did?
   _____
   _____
   _____

4. In terms of the overall job, is this employee's motivational level high or low?
   MOTIVATIONAL LEVEL: _____

5. What are the reasons you rated the employee's motivational level the way you did?
   _____
   _____
   _____

6. Based on your assessment of the employee's ability level (high or low) and motivational level (high or low), what is this employee's functional level?

F-1:	Low Ability and Low Motivation
F-2:	Low Ability and High Motivation
F-3:	High Ability and Low Motivation
F-4:	High Ability and High Motivation

Employee's F-level: _____

Next, notice that the initial factor assessed is the employee's ability level. Because the work has to be done, ability is often the key variable. Regardless of motivation, if the employee does not have the knowledge and skills to do the job, direction is clearly needed. Most supervisors, therefore, start with an assessment of the employee's ability level followed by an assessment of the motivational level.

Look at the ability level of your employee. Can the employee do the job? Are there skills or abilities that the employee is clearly lacking? The bottom line is that you are totally confident that even if you weren't there your employee could do the job without supervision. If the employee can do this, then the ability level is high. If not, then it is low.

With motivation the bottom-line question is, "On the tasks the employee knows how to do, is it reasonably certain that they would get done if I were not around?" If the answer is no, your employee has low motivation. If the answer is yes, your employee has high motivation. As you move forward in making a final determination of the employee's functional level, remember two simple rules.

1. *Document, document, document.* Substantiate your position. Your goal is to prove to yourself and to your employee the accuracy of your assessment of the employee's functional level.

2. *If you are not sure, be conservative.* If you are not sure that an employee has ability, assume it is low until you are comfortable that it is high. Let's face it. If you are about to board a plane, you wouldn't want to suddenly learn that the mechanic who had just fixed the plane had been given the benefit of the doubt on ability by his or her supervisor.

If you completed your assessment, were reasonably conservative, and documented your position, the next step is pretty easy: determine the functional level of your challenging employees.

F-1: Low Ability/Low Motivation

F-2: Low Ability/High Motivation

F-3: High Ability/Low Motivation

F-4: High Ability/High Motivation

Now you are ready to determine their supervisory needs.

Step 2. Define Employees' Needs and Your Supervisory Goals

As you begin this step and find yourself unsure, you probably ought to redefine your most challenging employee and reassess the employee's functional level.

The Defining Your Employee's Needs form is designed to aid you in this process. It is not enough to know an employee's general needs; you need to know the specific needs. The Defining Your Employee's Needs form gives you the chance to focus on specific needs. Once you name the needs, they can be addressed. Look at Section 2: Ability Level. Determine what specific needs your employee has in terms of ability. If the employee has low ability and you clearly documented this fact, what specific skills or knowledge is needed to remedy this? List all of them in order of their importance to the person's job.

Even if the employee has high ability, you still need to do this exercise. Although most jobs change gradually, they may still require the employee to learn new skills or knowledge. This is the time to identify that.

You approach motivation the same way—discover specifically what needs the employee has or why he or she is unmotivated. If the employee is an F-4 employee with high motivation, you still must fill out this section; it is especially important to identify this employee's motivational needs. You will quickly find that these needs relate to the employee's personal and professional development.

Once you have defined the employee's supervisory needs, it is an easy step to determine what your supervisory goals ought to be. They are simply a clarification of your efforts to respond to the employee's supervisory needs. For example, this is the same rationale used with students. If your fourth grader brings home a report card with four As and a D in math, you don't say "Let's provide more academic support to my child and start helping him or her with English." While you would cetainly praise your child for the four As, you are not going to help your child with English when the trouble is with math. Your goal is to assist your child in the subjects in which the child is weak. It's the same way with supervision.

Section 4 on the Defining Your Employee's Needs form pro-

Defining Your Employee's Needs

1. Employee's name _____
2. Ability level
   a. What is the employee's ability level? Low ____ High____
   b. What does the employee specifically need in response to his/her present ability level?
      1. _____
      2. _____
      3. _____
      4. _____
      5. _____

3. Motivation level
   a. What is the employee's motivation level? Low ____ High____
   b. What does the employee need in response to his/her motivation level?
      1. _____
      2. _____
      3. _____
      4. _____
      5. _____

4. Supervisory goals
   Based on your understanding of the employee's supervisory needs, what are your specific supervisory goals?
      1. _____
      2. _____
      3. _____
      4. _____
      5. _____

vides space to make your goals clear. Remember that if you know where you are going, you'll be able to figure out how to get there. Now you are ready to move into the actual supervision of your challenging employee. You've done your homework, have accurately assessed and documented the employee's functional level, and determined the supervisory needs and supervisory goals. You are ready to target your supervisory efforts to respond to the employee's needs.

Step 3. Clarify Your Assessment with Challenging Employees

The bad news is that this is probably the most difficult step in the process, particularly if you are supervising an F-1 or an F-3 employee. As you recall, you are letting the F-1 employee know that he or she has not demonstrated either appropriate levels of ability or motivation for the job. While the employee may realize that this is true, it is still difficult to hear. The employee may become defensive and you are likely to get some kind of reaction.

The F-3 employee is of equal concern. Since most F-3 employees regressed from an F-4 functional level, you are telling them they have lost something. Their performance is not what it used to be. To be told that their performance is sliding is not easy.

Supervisors must show some concern for employee feelings, and approach them with sensitivity, respect, and honesty both as employees and as people. When supervising your challenging employee or any employee, apply one of the Golden Rules of Supervision: treat each person with the same respect and sensitivity that you would like supervisors to use with you. Honesty from our supervisors is something everyone values.

In applying step three, the tendency is to focus on F-1 and F-3 employees because they are the two levels who will hear that their performance is slipping.

Again, document! The more facts that you document in your assessment, the easier your presentation will be. Show concrete examples that led you to make this assessment.

Your goal at this juncture in the process is to present enough substantiation to prove your point, but not enough to cause overkill. You want to explain why you see your employees at a particular functional level in order to support your rationale for the kinds of supervisory support you will be providing. If your challenging employees agree that they are functioning at a specific level, they are much more likely to agree with your supervisory goals and approach.

The Supervisory Goals Form provides you with some parameters for approaching any employee. It asks you to recognize that all employees strive to maintain some level of self-esteem and self-respect and that employees should be supervised in a manner that recognizes that. The form covers four issues that you need to consider when meeting with your challenging employee. You should

1. Acknowledge the strengths and contributions that the employee has made at work. Remember that even your F-1 employee has some strengths.
2. Acknowledge the employee's specific areas of weakness.
3. Provide clear documentation to substantiate your position.
4. Clearly state what your supervisory goals will be and how you intend to fulfill them.

It is important to view supervision as a communication rather than a monologue. Allow your employees the opportunity to

---

Supervisory Goals Form

1. Employee's name   _____

2. What are the major strengths or contributions that the employee has made to the workforce?   _____
   _____
   _____
   _____

3. What are the major weaknesses, issues, or problems with which the employee needs support?   _____
   _____
   _____
   _____
   _____

4. What are your supervisory goals with this employee?   _____
   _____
   _____

discuss, even challenge, your assessment. Listen carefully. If they bring up new information, acknowledge it. Be open to reconsidering your assessment if substantial new information comes to light. Normally, however, if you've done a good job documenting what you observed, you will probably maintain your original assessment and goals. And if you and your employee still cannot agree, remember one of the key rules of the Functional Management Model:

> If the supervisor and the employee are not in agreement on the supervisor's assessment of the employee's functional level, the final decision is that of the supervisor.

Previous chapters made it clear why this must be so. You, as a supervisor, can't take a chance. If there is any question about an employee's ability or motivation, you must assume that the employee is weak in ability and lacking in motivation—and supervise the employee more closely. If after a period of time, the employee proves able to come through, you can reassess your position and rate the employee at a higher functional level and adjust your supervisory approach accordingly.

Now that you and your challenging employee have a clear sense of your assessment and goals, you are now ready to supervise the employee in the best way possible.

Step 4. Develop and Initiate a Specific Supervisory Approach

It's time to follow through on your commitments. The Supervisor's Strategy Form provides you with an excellent way to begin targeting your supervisory efforts. Optimal supervision occurs when you respond to or address the specific needs of the employee (see the third question on the form). If you've done a good job in steps one, two, and three, you should have a clear sense of what those needs are. If you can name them, you can address them.

How will you address those needs? Once you have determined an employee's functional level, you should know what supervisory approach to use.

Supervisor's Strategy Form

1. Employee's name _____

2. Functional level _____ Supervisory approach _____

3. What specific employee needs will you address? _____

   _____

   _____

   _____

   _____

4. What forms of specific supervisory behaviors will you provide?

   a. Direction _____

   _____

   _____

   _____

   b. Work-specific support _____

   _____

   _____

   _____

   c. Personal and professional development support _____

   _____

   _____

F-1 employees need high direction and extensive work-specific support.

F-2 employees need high direction, high work-specific support, and minimal personal and professional development support.

F-3 employees need low direction, low work-specific support, and high personal and professional development support.

F-4 employees need low direction and extensive personal and professional development support.

Knowing which supervisory approach to use is not enough. It's too general. For optimal supervision, you must know exactly what you are going to do within each of the three supervisory behaviors. You must have well-thought-out, distinct strategies. You need to look at each of the three behaviors first.

Directive behavior.   Exactly what are you going to do to respond to an employee's supervisory needs? What directions do you think you should provide? What types of training will you provide? What, if any, efforts should you initiate to coordinate your employee's efforts? Are there specific things your employee needs to know concerning when work should be done? In short, what types of direction do you need to provide?

Work-specific support.   Does the employee need extensive performance feedback? Are there specific areas of performance on which you need to provide feedback? Do you believe that this employee needs intensive encouragement and support or other types of support?

Personal and professional development support.   Are there specific ways that you should respond to the employee's personal needs? What can you realistically do to respond to these needs? What about their professional needs? New learning opportunities? Take charge of a project? New responsibilities?

You will not have a broad range of actions under each of these behaviors. Much depends on the type of supervisory approach you use. You will obviously have a great deal more directive behavior for your F-1 or F-2 employees than for your F-3 or F-4 employees. Conversely, you should be putting much greater emphasis on personal and professional development for your F-3 or F-4 employees. What you do and the number of specific actions you initiate will differ according to the functional level of the employee. How do you know if you are really effective? That's where the final step comes in.

Step 5: Monitor, Document, and Refine Your Supervisory Efforts

You won't know if you are being an effective supervisor unless you monitor the results of your supervision and document what is happening. You can improve your efforts through refinement based on what you learned from monitoring and documenting the progress of your employee.

Step five is important for a number of reasons. First, only by monitoring the efforts of your employee can you measure or assess the growth or changes that may be taking place. Monitoring the employee's performance allows you to determine whether your supervisory strategies are helpful or not as effective as you had hoped.

Second, monitoring puts you in position to refine your efforts. Supervisors learn from their experiences. By being aware of what works and what doesn't work with a particular employee, you can reinforce effective strategies and change those that aren't. In this way, you can be a more effective supervisor.

Third, by feeding back your findings to employees, you give them the opportunity to know how they are doing, a clear sense of the areas where they need improvement, and the opportunity to focus their energies in these areas. Documentation is important; the more accurately you document and substantiate an employee's progress or lack of it in a particular area, the easier it will be to get the employee to recognize that more needs to be done in that area. You and your employee mutually gain because you both share the goal of wanting the employee to succeed on the job.

Often a supervisor and employee talk about what support has helped and what hasn't. If you both agree, the process of jointly coming up with new strategies will dramatically improve the chances that the supervisor's efforts respond effectively to the employee's needs.

Documentation also reinforces an employee's progress more effectively. Supervisors can't give negative feedback alone; they should be giving positive feedback whenever appropriate. Positive feedback reinforces the employee's progress and sense of your awareness and caring.

This leads to the fourth reason why this step is so important. When you monitor and document an employee's progress and provide regular feedback, you give the employee an important message: I'm doing a lot of work defining your supervisory needs and my supervisory goals, so I'm going to follow up on my efforts.

When employees see how serious you are about following up on your commitments, they will quickly realize how important this is and how committed you are to helping them. It certainly gives them an incentive to work more closely with you.

The Employee Monitor and Review Form provides you with the opportunity to focus on monitoring, documenting, and refining your efforts. Question two asks you to identify exactly how you are going to do this. Are you going to directly observe the employee? Get feedback from others? Review reports? Test for quality? If you accept how critical the monitoring of your employee's functioning and progress is, then you need to know exactly how to do the monitoring. Will you work with the employee and directly observe him? Is this really possible or just wishful thinking on your part? Many supervisors, particularly those who are frustrated, intend to monitor the employee's performance very tightly, particularly F-1

Employee Monitor and Review Form

1. Employee's name _____

2. How will you monitor and document your employee's progress?

   a. _____

   b. _____

   c. _____

   d. _____

3. What positive or negative changes have you been able to verify and document? _____

   _____

   _____

   _____

   _____

4. When will you provide the employee with supervision and feedback on his/her performance? Give exact times and dates. It is preferable to have a regular day and time. _____

   _____

5. What has worked for you with this employee? _____

   _____

   _____

6. What has not worked with this employee? _____

   _____

   _____

---

employees. Sometimes they begin by working very closely with the employee but soon realize that this level of intensity cannot be maintained. So they start cutting back the time spent with the employee, often leaving the employee confused about why the supervisor's support is being withdrawn.

Be realistic in monitoring an employee's performance. How often are you monitoring the employee? Daily? Biweekly? Weekly? Something else? How much time can you afford to spend monitoring the employee? Will some of your monitoring come from others? Are there reports that you can use? Are there other methods that you can use to monitor the employee's functioning?

The vehicles you use to monitor the employee also are intended to help you document the employee's performance. Question three asks you to document what you observe. During formal supervision sessions it is of paramount importance that you provide feedback on how the employee is doing. Documentation will make that feedback more effective and more helpful to the employee. There can be no confusion over what you are talking about.

Question four asks you to identify a time for feedback. Optimal supervision is achieved when you have a fixed meeting time with employees for discussion and feedback. If employees know that every Tuesday at 3:00 P.M. or the second and fourth Thursday of each month at 10:30 A.M. they will receive formal supervision, they become much more aware of their functioning and performance. They know that this is the time when they learn how they are doing, discuss problems, and receive support from their supervisor.

Finally, in monitoring the functioning of your challenging employee, you will discover that neither supervision nor supervisors are stagnant. You should be learning something about yourself. You should become aware of what works for you and what doesn't.

What have you noticed in looking at your efforts? Are you doing all the talking? Are you listening enough? What have you done that has been particularly helpful to the employee? What have you observed that works for you? What hasn't? What would help you to be a more effective supervisor? Questions five and six ask you to look at yourself seriously and find out what you've learned.

MAKING IT WORK

Will everything work out perfectly? Will everyone live happily ever after? Will your most challenging employee say to you "You're the best supervisor in the world?" Probably not. You are bound to run into problems. If you didn't, this employee would not be your "most challenging employee." But you have begun a process that clearly targets the primary needs of the employee.

To make it work, you need to be consistent. You must follow through on your commitments. If you say you are going to do something, you have to do it. The employee must know that you are predictable. You also must be methodical and thorough in your initial analysis. Your effectiveness in applying the later steps of the Functional Management Model depends on your effectiveness in the initial steps.

You also need to be flexible and willing to respond to new realities as they emerge. You and your employee are going to learn and change from this process. After all, your ultimate goal is to get the employee to change. So if your employee changes it stands to reason that it may be appropriate for you to change your approach, strategies, or actions in response.

Finally, you need to be patient and realistic. The employee you identified has probably been in his or her present level for some time. I remember hoping that my graduate school professors would give me some magic words that I could use with my employees so that they would start functioning at an F-4 level. No such luck. There are no magic words that you can say that will result in an immediate change.

How long will it take before employees begin making the initial shift? It depends on several factors. How long the employees have functioned like this. How receptive they are to change. The complexity of the job. Your effectiveness as a supervisor. Your ability to accurately assess their supervisory needs. These, with an unlimited number of other variables, will influence how soon you can expect to see results.

But you will be effective if you are patient; if you do a thorough job assessing your employees' supervisory needs; if you accurately target your supervisory approach, strategies, and action to their needs; and if you appropriately monitor, document, and refine your efforts. Your employees will gain from the experience. They will grow and mature, and then have the potential of becoming or remaining F-4 employees.

Chapter Eleven

Questions and Answers
Responding to Questions People Ask Most

W hen I began this book, I had one goal in mind: to present my readers with a supervisory management model that not only works but is easy to use. Implicit in this goal was my intent to present the model in a manner that made it easy to learn.

This may sound easy, but my experience researching the available literature indicates that this can be a difficult thing for an author to achieve. What may seem straightforward to those who design and provide training for a particular model or concept can be confusing to the reader or participant. I also know that what may sound practical and reasonable when presented in a book or in a training can suddenly become a real problem when you try to apply it. Everything seems to be going well, but then something comes up that doesn't quite fit the model. You have questions that you don't know how to answer.

So, what should you do? If you are trying to apply something you learned from a book, you might review the sections of the book you're unclear about. Perhaps you'll find a key point that you missed. If it was something you were taught in a training session, you might contact someone you think has a better understanding of the model, a colleague who took the training or even the trainer. In short, you do what you can to get your questions answered.

The Functional Management Model is named that for a good reason; it is functional—a supervisory model specifically designed to be clearly understood and easy to use. It also is a model with possible far-reaching effects in an organization. It is a tool that allows supervisors to approach systematically a variety of problems within the workplace. Inevitably situations will arise that leave questions with those applying the model. In anticipation of your questions I have included answers to questions on various aspects of the model and its application.

Answering questions about the model is easy in training sessions. It's a little harder when you're reading a book. How do you get your questions answered when it's just you and the book at 10:00 P.M. on a Sunday?

To help you better understand the model and to increase your ability to effectively apply it, I have identified the most frequently asked questions and grouped them under the appropriate categories. The same types of questions were asked over and over by training participants regardless of the fields they may work in. They tend to fall into one of three categories:

1. Determining an employee's functional level.
2. The three supervisory behaviors.
3. Applying the Functional Management Model.

I hope that this chapter will provide answers to your questions concerning either understanding or applying the Functional Management Model.

QUESTIONS ON EMPLOYEE FUNCTIONAL LEVELS

It is appropriate to begin by focusing on questions related to employees' functional levels because the application of the Functional Management Model requires that you first look at the employee. Determine the employee's ability level followed by the motivational level. Finally, based on your assessment, determine the employee's functional level. You will recall that only by knowing how well the employee is functioning are you in a position to know how to best supervise that employee.

Is "attitude" ability or motivation?   We've all run across people with "bad attitudes." They don't get along with anyone. They're moody and snap at people. At other times they are aloof. Employees like this are often viewed as rude and as major detractors from team morale. In all but the rarest of cases, this attitude is a reflection of motivation, not ability. Most people know how to be polite and how to get along with people. They also know when they are being moody. The problem is that they choose to behave this way. This attitude does not help them and certainly affects the overall morale of the team in the workplace. In concrete terms, you need to point out examples of their bad attitude and communicate what you expect. Your next challenge is to motivate them to do what you want them to do.

It's usually uncomfortable discussing attitude with an employee. But if you are aware of the employee's problems in this area, then you must discuss it. How aggressively you decide to deal with the problem relates directly to how serious you perceive it to be. Remember it is not only the employee you are dealing with but also the morale of the whole team. Be direct with this employee. Bring up clear, documented examples. Point out incidents as soon as possible after they occur. Let the employee know what you expect. Work with your F-3 employees particularly, to identify ways to increase their overall positive motivation.

Don't be confused if the issue turns out to be ability rather than motivation. The same process works for attitude problems related to ability. The key is to be clear and to monitor the problem tightly.

How can you help an F-1 or F-2 employee learn the necessary skills on the job? This question has two answers. The first has to do with the nature of the job. What you do with an employee differs according to the complexity of the job. Complex jobs take more time to learn than simple jobs. As a supervisor, you must adjust the time you allow a person to learn a new job and provide a level of support based on the complexity of the job.

The second answer involves the learning style of the employee. Some employees learn best by observing, some by listening, and others by hands-on experience. While you want to incorporate all learning styles in your training approach, your efforts will be enhanced if you determine the preferred learning style of the employee and use that style when possible. Don't be afraid to ask employees how they learn best. Together you might find ways to help them learn the needed skills.

When should you give up on an employee? The politically correct answer to this question is that you never give up on an employee! While ideally this should be your attitude, in reality you may have an employee who neither can nor will do what is expected.

Very often, this is an F-1 employee. Give this employee ample time and opportunity to learn the job, but don't wait too long. Your initial goal is to do everything possible to help an F-1 employee learn the skills and gain the motivation to do the job. At the same time, however, you need to set realistic benchmarks and clear timelines for what the employee must do to succeed on the job, and when this should be accomplished. Remember that F-1 employees affect the norm, morale, and ultimately the credibility of your team. If they are not performing and don't meet your benchmarks and timelines, then in fairness to them and to other members of your team, you must initiate a progressive termination procedure.

Do employees normally function at one level? Employees tend to have a predominant functional level. They do not, however, function strictly at one level. An employee may be predominantly an F-4 employee, but tend to function at an F-3 or even F-1 level when doing paperwork. Even your least functional employees may have certain work-related skills where they function at an F-4 level.

Employees normally demonstrate consistent high or low ability and motivation levels. As a supervisor, your challenge is to identify those levels and supervise the employees accordingly.

Is there a hard and fast rule that tells me when to rate an employee high or low on ability or motivation? Sorry! There is no firm rule. The advice to you is to be conservative. If you're not sure, rate that employee's ability or motivation level as low until you have verifiable documentation that would make you feel comfortable in giving a high rating.

Should you use the language of the model—F-1, F-2, F-3, and F-4? This is by far the most hotly debated question I have been asked. Those who favor using the language of the Functional Management Model say it conveys information to others rapidly and effectively. You don't need to spend a lot of time explaining what you mean. Supervisors who know the model know, for example, what an F-3 employee is, and they can more quickly provide you with suggestions.

Those who argue against using the language of the model say that its terms label a person and do not allow for a more in-depth assessment. They argue that the people who know the model immediately move to their most typical employee at any given functional level and use this person as their image of all employees at that level. Instead of looking at employees as individuals with particular strengths and weaknesses, supervisors simply label employees, e.g., "He's an F-3 employee."

The best response is to acknowledge both arguments. It is true that using the language of the Functional Management Model makes it easier to express your assessment of that person's functional level. It is also true that this shorthand version of expressing a person's functional level obviously does not convey the complexity of issues related to a person's ability or motivation.

The best way for supervisors to use the language is to understand the context in which it is being used. When discussing employees or Functional Management Model concepts in general, the language of the model can be used both appropriately and effectively. However, to convey a more detailed profile and analysis of a specific employee's functioning on the job, you need to present substantiated information.

Should you tell employees the functional level at which you see them?   Yes, absolutely! There is no hedging on this question. Your behavior toward your employees and how you supervise them depends on your perception of them. If you see them as intelligent and highly motivated, and having the necessary skills and ability, you will treat and supervise them in one way. If you see them as slow or having limited skills and motivation, you will probably treat them another way.

Consider the following situation. You believe your employee is functioning at the F-1 or F-2 level. The employee does not agree and feels that an F-4 level is appropriate. You provide lots of direction—training, coordination, and tight supervision. The employee in turn, wonders why you are checking up all the time and finds your intense direction and work-specific support more than a little irritating.

But if you and your employee agree on his or her specific functional level, the employee would understand and expect the types of supervisory support that you are providing. Even if the employee did not agree with your assessment, he or she could at least understand why you are using a specific supervisory approach.

Maybe the easiest way to clarify my position is by having you look at yourself and ask the following question:

> If you know that your boss has analyzed your work performance and has made a judgment about your functional level, do you want to know what it is?

The vast majority of supervisors and managers I have interviewed answered this question with a resounding yes. Most people—supervisors and employees—want to know how they have been assessed so that they can better understand how they are perceived and why they are supervised in a certain way. It also gives them the opportunity to identify what they must do to progress to an F-4 level. If they believe themselves to be at this level already, then they have the information at hand to convince their supervisor as well.

QUESTIONS ON THE THREE SUPERVISORY BEHAVIORS

Questions related to supervisory behaviors normally come up as managers begin applying the behaviors. Am I doing too much? What specific personal and professional development support should I provide? How do I provide this employee with appropriate work-specific support? What can I do to motivate this employee? However, very often other questions emerge that focus on the more general application of the Functional Management Model and could apply to any manager in any industry.

How does the provision of direction differ among the four functional levels? It is not simply the amount and intensity of direction that are given. Obviously the amount of time providing training, skill development, and other forms of direction is normally far greater with F-1 and F-2 employees.

Direction also differs in content among the four functional levels. For example, much of the content of the direction provided F-1 and F-2 employees is skill development. F-3 and F-4 employees already have the skills so their direction content centers on coordination, information sharing, and identifying future efforts that need to take place.

Supervisors obviously need to spend far less time providing direction to the F-3 and F-4 employee. This reality is clearly represented in the supervisory approach component of the Functional Management Chart.

Do F-1 employees need personal and professional development support? Yes, all employees need some degree of this kind of support. But the model may surprise you; F-1 employees are getting it. The definition of personal and professional development support includes the provision of skills and knowledge that help in the development of an employee.

Because F-1 employees lack much of the knowledge and many of the skills they need to do the job, providing them with training and skill development enhances their personal and professional development. Some level of personal and professional development is implied within the directive behavior every time training is given.

Do F-4 employees sometimes need work-specific support? Of course. A degree of work-specific support is implied in personal and professional development support. When you focus heavily on employees' personal and professional development, you are also communicating your recognition of their contributions and accomplishments. That's why you are so interested in supporting their growth.

What you are not doing is providing reinforcement on work employees have done successfully for years. While periodically acknowledging their consistency—employees like to know that their manager isn't taking them for granted—managers should support employee development as a primary vehicle to acknowledge their work.

Supervisors ask, "How do I know what is the best form of personal and professional development support to provide?" You don't, at least initially. The goal is to respond to the personal development and professional development of a specific employee. What is a developmental opportunity for one employee may be dull and certainly unmotivating to another.

You learn what the best form of personal and professional development support is by working with specific employees to find out what developmental opportunities they value. What personal goals does the employee have? What activities are of interest? What specific professional trainings or opportunities, if any, would the employee like to take advantage of?

Your challenge is to work jointly with individual employees to identify developmental opportunities that are of value to them yet are also possible within the financial and operational realities of your organization.

QUESTIONS ON APPLYING THE FUNCTIONAL MANAGEMENT MODEL

Knowing about the functional levels and supervisory approaches was not always enough. I found that participants in training sessions and workshops had numerous questions about applying the model and about optimal supervision. The following are responses to some of the most frequently asked questions.

How often should I supervise my employees? Unfortunately, this question has no simple answer. How often a supervisor should hold a formal one-on-one meeting depends on the job, the needs of the employee, and a number of other factors that vary from job to job. Some jobs require intense supervisory support and regularly scheduled supervisory meetings. Clinicians who work with troubled families or mentally ill adults often have regularly scheduled supervisory sessions two or more times a week. The intensity of the interaction and the need for a supervisor to check and support a clinician's work is essential to good clinical process. Intensive supervisory support also applies to some accounting, computer programming, or scientific jobs.

Other jobs normally do not require close supervision once employees have learned the job and proven themselves capable and motivated. A few examples are sales representatives, technicians, travel agents, claims adjusters, and college professors.

As a supervisor, you must be aware of the needs of your employees and the level of support they require. In jobs where the manager and employees are working together on a regular basis, feedback is often immediate. Since the supervisor sees the employees on a daily basis, it may be acceptable to meet with them as little as once a month. Where employees are more often on their own, regularly scheduled supervisory support is obviously needed. As the manager, you must make the final determination; the answers to two questions will help in that determination.

1. From the employee's perspective, how many hours of regularly scheduled supervision and support does the employee feel that he or she needs?

2. From your perspective as that employee's supervisor, what level of supervisory support must you provide to feel assured that the employee is functioning at an optimal level?

Use your assessment of your employee's needs as the minimal acceptable standard and go from there. This will give you an appropriate balance. If the employee feels that he or she needs more regularly scheduled supervision, work together to determine the appropriate level.

What shared goals should a supervisor have in supervising all levels of employees? While "what" a supervisor does with specific employees varies from employee to employee, within the same functional level supervisors tend to have one general goal for all employees. This goal is to help every employee evolve to an F-4 level or help F-4 employees maintain their motivation and commitment.

Some supervisors have argued that the goal should be to have a good cross-section of employees. That's not my perspective. I firmly believe that the goal is to get all employees to reach an F-4 functional level. The more employees you have at that level, the higher will be the achievement of your unit or department.

How does the Functional Management Model relate to total quality management (TQM)? One of the major questions that often arises concerns the implementation of a total quality management program. "How do I realistically involve my staff in the total quality effort? The Functional Management Model helps answer that question.

Many of the leading advocates of TQM programs propose a continuous improvement effort. Affecting every department and operation of the organization, continuous improvement efforts call for the active participation of all employees in the organization in continually seeking new and better ways to operate. Empowerment and involvement of all employees in the process are essential. How do you realistically involve all employees in the TQM effort?—through the Functional Management Model. You know that the Functional Management Model makes it clear that employees function at any one of four levels. Some employees need more direction and work-specific support while others need more personal and professional development support. When you consider the application of these realities to the development of a TQM program, how to involve employees more realistically becomes evident.

When empowering employees and involving them in the TQM program, it is apparent that all employees must have some basic skills in order for the program to be effective. These may be analytical, problem-identification, or problem-solving skills. Teaching all employees all the skills is neither realistic nor cost-effective. Therefore certain unique skills essential to the TQM effort need to be present in the organization, but do not need to be learned by all employees. These skills may include group facilitation skills, meeting skills, and outcome oriented planning. F-3 and F-4 employees are ideal candidates for learning unique skills.

The key to the individual relationship between TQM and the Functional Management Model is to clearly distinguish between basic and unique skills. By providing all employees with basic skills, you empower them and ensure that all of them have the knowledge and skills essential for helping the organization continually improve. By providing additional leadership skills to your F-3 and F-4 employees, you reward them for their previous accomplishments and motivate them by responding to their need for personal and professional development support.

Are there advantages to having the Functional Management Model integrated throughout an organization? Absolutely! When everyone in an organization is familiar with the Functional Management Model, supervisory and organizational relationships become clearer and easier to support.

Supervisors who use the Functional Management Model tend to be very clear on what skills people in specific jobs need. They monitor them more closely. They tend to be a lot more realistic and supportive in their supervisory efforts. Finally, they have a better understanding of when and how to support the personal and professional development of each employee.

On an individual level, the Functional Management Model helps supervisors to become more sensitive and responsive to the unique needs and potential of each employee. Supervisors develop a solid appreciation for how to best support, motivate, and supervise each of them.

The integration of the Functional Management Model allows organizations to develop strategies and policies that are far more supportive of supervisors and employees alike. Personnel policies are often creative approaches to the personal and professional development needs of employees, e.g., flextime, training days, development days, and quality of work life plans. Evaluations include a formal professional development plan for each employee. Supervisory training sessions are held regularly so that supervisors learn new and more effective ways to deal with their employees at specific functional levels.

Finally, when employees and supervisors at all levels of the organization know the Functional Management Model, discussions on how to support employees become more focused and more effective. The integration of the model has the potential to truly enhance all aspects of the personnel functioning in the organization.

A FINAL WORD

I believe that the supervisory work of managers of organizations throughout the country is the glue that holds organizations together and is the foundation for the future of the organization. Strong, supportive supervision leads to strong organizations—organizations that are focused, dynamic, and continually driven to help each employee achieve his or her optimal level of performance.

When supervisors know how to respond effectively to the supervisory needs of each of their employees, they are more confident and more competent in their job. Better yet, employees feel more supported, respected, and recognized for their individual strengths and weaknesses. The Functional Management Model provides you with a proven supervisory management model that works for both supervisors and employees.

Bibliography

The development of a new model of supervisory management doesn't just fall out of the sky. It is the culmination of learning and insights gained from many sources. Three kinds of sources have stood out: personal experience in the workplace, training sessions with supervisors, and published works.

The most obvious source derives from what I have learned from supervisors, colleagues, and employees. Their feedback shaped and solidifed my view of how to best support and supervise employees. There is no question that the development of the Functional Management Model was partially shaped from these experiences.

The second source of input and guidance was gleaned from the real-life experience of people who know the most about supervision. Over the years, I have been involved in training and educational programs with thousands of supervisors and managers throughout the country. Their thirst for knowledge and their commitment to finding the best way to do their job and to support their employees led to many lively discussions and further refinement of the model.

The third source derives from previously published works on management-related issues. As an avid reader and researcher, I have been deeply impressed and influenced by the extensive writings of theorists and practioners. Some have focused on supervision, others on philosophy and theory, and still others on the effect of large-scale management practices on personnel management. All have shaped my perspective on supervision and have guided and enhanced the practicality and responsiveness of the Functional Management Model.

It is impossible to identify every book and article that has influenced my thinking, but I can identify some of the more recent works that have played a role in helping to reflect upon and refine the model. The bibliography is divided into four major parts: management philosophy, culture and teamwork, total quality management, and supervision and leadership.

MANAGEMENT PHILOSOPHY

How managers should view and consider their overall organizational management is covered in works on management practice and theory. These books go far beyond simply personnel supervision, reviewing in many cases every aspect of the organization, its strategies, and structure. These books are relevant to the Functional Management Model because they reinforce the importance of supporting and empowering employees while making it clear that the future of an organization depends on the vitality, motivation, and commitment of the workforce.

Drucker, Peter F. *Management: Tasks, Responsibilities, Practices.* New York: Harper & Row, 1973.

Peters, Thomas J., and Waterman, Robert H., Jr. *In Search of Excellence.* New York: Harper & Row, 1982.

Peters, Tom. *Liberation Management.* New York: Alfred A. Knopf, 1992.

Waterman, Robert H., Jr. *The Renewal Factor.* New York: Bantam Books, 1987.

CULTURE AND TEAMWORK

One of the important aspects of an organization's culture is its view of and involvement with teams. In some organizational cultures, teams are not valued. Others strongly support the empowerment of employees and the use of teams. In this section are books that will help you better appreciate the importance of organizational culture and the recognition that effective supervision can gain from and enhance the development of teams.

Deal, Terrence E., and Kennedy, Allan A. *Corporate Cultures.* Reading, MA: Addison-Wesley, 1982.

Hampden-Turner, Charles. *Creating Corporate Culture: From Discord to Harmony.* Reading, MA: Addison-Wesley, 1992.

Hastings, Colin; Bixby, Peter; and Chaudhry-Lawton, Rani. *The Super-team Solution: Successful Teamworking in Organizations.* San Diego: University Associates, 1987.

Hirschhorn, Larry. *Managing in the New Team Environment: Skills, Tools, and Methods.* Reading, MA: Addison-Wesley, 1991.

Lawler, Edward E. III. *High-Involvement Management.* San Francisco: Jossey-Bass, 1986.

Orsburn, Jack D.; Moran, Linda; Musselwhite, Ed; and Zenger, John H. *Self-Directed Work Teams: The New American Challenge.* Homewood, IL: Business One Irwin, 1990.

Pascarella, Perry, and Frohman, Mark A. *The Purpose-Driven Organization: Unleashing the Power of Direction and Commitment.* San Francisco: Jossey-Bass, 1989.

TOTAL QUALITY MANAGEMENT

Total quality management is more than a set of management principles and practices. It is a philosophical approach to management that emphasizes the empowerment of employees and commitment to absolute quality and to continuous improvement. Because TQM is a profound movement that has gained widespread acceptance by nearly all industries and is becoming a norm rather than a philosophy, the list of books on the subject is separated from that on management philosophy. The list includes key works that will help you understand how the Functional Management Model addresses the question, "How do we most effectively involve all of our staff in the TQM effort?"

Albrecht, Karl, and Zemke, Ron. *Service America! Doing Business in the New Economy.* Homewood, IL: Dow-Jones Irwin, 1985.

Bowles, Jerry, and Hammond, Joshua. *Beyond Quality: How 50 Winning Companies Use Continuous Improvement.* New York: G. P. Putnam's Sons, 1991.

Ciampa, Dan. *Total Quality: A User's Guide for Implementation.* Reading, MA: Addison-Wesley, 1992.

Crosby, Philip B. *Quality Is Free: The Art of Making Quality Certain.* New York: McGraw-Hill, 1979.

Davidow, William H., and Uttal, Bro. *Total Customer Service: The Ultimate Weapon.* New York: Harper & Row, 1989.

Ishikawa, Kaoru. *What Is Total Quality Control? The Japanese Way.* Englewood Cliffs, NJ: Prentice-Hall, 1985.

Jablonski, Joseph R. *Implementing Total Quality Management: An Overview.* San Diego: Pfeiffer, 1991.

Lele, Milind M., and Sheth, Jagdish N. *The Customer Is Key: Gaining an Unbeatable Advantage through Customer Satisfaction.* New York: John Wiley & Sons, 1987.

Whiteley, Richard C. *The Customer-Driven Company: Moving from Talk to Action.* Reading, MA: Addison-Wesley, 1991.

Zemke, Ron, and Bell, Chip R. *Service Wisdom: Creating and Maintaining the Customer Service Edge.* Minneapolis, MN: Lakewood Books, 1989.

SUPERVISION AND LEADERSHIP

Many of these works are not traditional supervision books but books that discuss the importance of leadership and relationships among people. They provide a wonderful foundation on how to be a more effective leader and how to effectively supervise and motivate staff.

Austin, Michael J. *Supervisory Management for the Human Services.* Englewood Cliffs, NJ: Prentice-Hall, 1981.

Beck, Arthur C., and Hillman, Ellis D. *Positive Management Practices.* San Francisco: Jossey-Bass, 1986.

Bennis, Warren, and Nanus, Burt. *Leaders: The Strategies for Taking Charge.* New York: Harper & Row, 1985.

Cassell, Clark C.; Knight, Mark A.; and McGuire, Janet L., eds. *Contemporary Directions in Human Resource Management.* Rockville, MD: National Council of Community Mental Health Centers, 1990.

Covey, Stephen R. *The Seven Habits of Highly Effective People.* New York: Fireside, 1990.

Davis, Louis E., and Cherns, Albert B., eds. *The Quality of Working Life,* Vol. 1, *Problems, Prospects and the State of the Art.* New York: Free Press, 1975.

DePree, Max. *Leadership Is an Art.* New York: Dell, 1989.

Hersey, Paul. *The Situational Leader.* New York: Warner Books, 1984.

Hersey, Paul, and Blanchard, Kenneth H. *Management of Organizational Behavior: Utilizing Human Resources.* 5th ed. Englewood Cliffs, NJ: Prentice Hall, 1988.

Kirkpatrick, Donald L. *A Practical Guide for Supervisory Training and Development.* Reading, MA: Addison-Wesley, 1971.

Lao-Tsu. *Tao Te Ching.* Feng, Gia-Fu, and English, Jane, trans. New York: Vintage Books, 1972.

Locke, Edwin A., and Latham, Gary P. *Goal Setting: A Motivational Technique that Works!* Englewood Cliffs, NJ: Prentice-Hall, 1984.

Mink, Oscar G.; Shultz, James M.; and Mink, Barbara P. *Developing and Managing Open Organizations.* San Diego: Learning Concepts, 1979.

Nanus, Burt. *Visionary Leadership.* San Francisco: Jossey-Bass, 1992.

Odiorne, George S. *The Human Side of Management.* Lexington, MA: Lexington Books, 1987.

Peck, M. Scott. *The Road Less Traveled.* New York: Simon & Schuster, 1978.

Ritvo, Roger A., and Sargent, Alice G., eds. *The NTL Managers' Handbook.* Arlington, VA: NTL Institute, 1983.

Schein, Edgar H. *Organizational Culture and Leadership.* San Francisco: Jossey-Bass, 1985.

Smedes, Lewis B. *A Pretty Good Person: What It Takes to Live with Courage, Gratitude and Integrity.* San Francisco: HarperCollins, 1990.

Taylor, Frederick W. *The Principles of Scientific Management.* 1911. Reprint. New York: W. W. Norton, 1967.

Ullrich, Robert A. *Motivation Methods that Work.* New York: Prentice Hall, 1981.

Wiles, Jon, and Bondi, Joseph. *Supervision: A Guide to Practice.* Columbus, OH: Charles E. Merrill, 1980.

Endnotes

CHAPTER ONE

1. Institutions such as the Malcolm Baldridge Award, a national award for organizational excellence, further challenges organizations and encourages businesses to aspire to higher ideals and expectations of themselves.
2. *Boston Globe*, March 26, 1989.
3. Personal correspondence to author from Frank Popoff.
4. *Boston Globe*, April 30, 1991.

CHAPTER TWO

1. Michael Verespej, "People: The Only Sustainable Edge," *Industry Week* (July 1, 1991):19–21.
2. *Fortune* (November 4, 1991):204
3. Frederick Herzberg, *The Motivation to Work* (New York: John Wiley and Sons, 1959).
4. Douglas McGregor, *The Human Side of Enterprise* (New York: McGraw-Hill, 1966).
5. Thomas J. Peters and Robert H. Waterman, Jr., *In Search of Excellence* (New York: Harper & Row, 1982):238.
6. Personal correspondence to author from James Kinnear.
7. Personal interview by author with Diana Buckley.
8. Philip Crosby, *Quality is Free* (New York: McGraw-Hill, 1980); W. E. Deming, *Out of Crisis* (Cambridge: MIT Press, 1986); A. Feigenbaum, *Total Quality Control* (New York: John Wiley and Sons, 1986); J. Juran Juran, *On Leadership for Quality* (New York: Free Press, 1988).
9. Jerry Bowles and Joshua Hammond, *Beyond Quality* (New York: G. P. Putnam's Sons, 1991):157–158.

CHAPTER THREE

1. Karl Albrecht and Ron Zemke, *Service America! Doing Business in the New Economy* (Homewood, IL: Dow Jones-Irwin, 1985):107.
2. Kaoru Ishikawa, *What is Total Quality Control? The Japanese Way* (Englewood Cliffs, NJ: Prentice-Hall, 1985):97.
3. Robert Levering, Milton Moskowitz, and Michael Katz, *The Hundred Best Companies to Work for in America* (New York: Plume Publishing, 1985):223–226.
4. Max DePree, *Leadership Is an Art* (New York: Dell Publishing, 1989):25.
5. Anthony P. Carnevale et al, "Workplace Basics: The Skills Employers Want," *Training and Development Journal* (October 1988):24.

CHAPTER FOUR

1. Frederick W. Taylor, *The Principles of Scientific Management*. First published in 1911 (New York: W. W. Norton, 1967).
2. Fritz J. Rothlisberger and William J. Dickson, *Manager and the Worker* (Cambridge: Harvard University Press, 1939).
3. Douglas McGregor, *The Human Side of Enterprise* (New York: McGraw-Hill, 1960).
4. Paul Hersey and Kenneth H. Blanchard, *Management of Organizational Behavior*, 5th ed. (Englewood Cliffs, NJ: Prentice-Hall, 1988).

CHAPTER SIX

1. Karl Albrecht and Ron Zemke, *Service America: Doing Business in the New Economy* (Homewood, IL: Dow Jones-Irwin, 1985).
2. Karl Albrecht, *The Only Thing That Matters: Bringing the Power of the Customer into the Center of the Business* (New York: Harper Business Publishers, 1992):145.

CHAPTER EIGHT

1. *Personnel* 67, no. 9 (September 1990):12.
2. *Ibid.*
3. M. Scott Peck, *The Road Less Traveled* (New York: Simon and Schuster, 1978):30.

Index

Other excellent resources available from Irwin Professional Publishing . . .

LEADING TEAMS

Mastering the New Role

John H. Zenger, Ed Musselwhite, Kathleen Hurson, and Craig Perrin

Focuses specifically on the role of the leader as the key to long-term success. This book shows how managers can carve an enduring and vital position for themselves in a team environment. (275 pages)
ISBN 1-55623-894-0

UNLEASHING PRODUCTIVITY!

Your Guide to Unlocking the Secrets of Super Performance

Richard Ott with Martin Snead

This quick read to becoming more creative, productive, and satisfied shows how to recognize and remove productivity barriers. Packed with tips, techniques, and ideas that show how to get the most from their work force and themselves. (200 pages)
ISBN 1-55623-931-9

EMPOWERING EMPLOYEES THROUGH DELEGATION

Robert B. Nelson

Shows you how—along with *what* and *when*—to delegate effectively. This *Briefcase Book* will take the manager step-by-step through the process of delegating by communicating responsibility in a way that ensures all parties know exactly what is expected of them. (175 pages)
ISBN 1-55623-847-9

Available at fine bookstores and libraries everywhere.